**New Directions for
Institutional Research**

Gloria Crisp
EDITOR

# Student Veteran Data in Higher Education

Kevin Eagan

Lesley McBain

Kevin C. Jones

EDITORS

Number 171
Jossey-Bass
San Francisco

Student Veteran Data in Higher Education
Kevin Eagan, Lesley McBain, and Kevin C. Jones (eds.)
New Directions for Institutional Research, no. 171
Editor: Gloria Crisp

NEW DIRECTIONS FOR INSTITUTIONAL RESEARCH, (Print ISSN: 0271-0579; Online ISSN: 1536-075X), is published quarterly by Wiley Subscription Services, Inc., a Wiley Company, 111 River St., Hoboken, NJ 07030-5774 USA.

Postmaster: Send all address changes to NEW DIRECTIONS FOR INSTITUTIONAL RESEARCH, John Wiley & Sons Inc., C/O The Sheridan Press, PO Box 465, Hanover, PA 17331 USA.

## Information for subscribers

NEW DIRECTIONS FOR INSTITUTIONAL RESEARCH is published in 4 issues per year. Institutional subscription prices for 2017 are: Print & Online: US$461 (US), US$515 (Canada & Mexico), US$561 (Rest of World), €366 (Europe), £2890 (UK). Prices are exclusive of tax. Asia-Pacific GST, Canadian GST/HST and European VAT will be applied at the appropriate rates. For more information on current tax rates, please go to www.wileyonlinelibrary.com/tax-vat. The price includes online access to the current and all online backfiles to January 1st 2013, where available. For other pricing options, including access information and terms and conditions, please visit www.wileyonlinelibrary.com/access.

## Delivery Terms and Legal Title

Where the subscription price includes print issues and delivery is to the recipient's address, delivery terms are **Delivered at Place (DAP)**; the recipient is responsible for paying any import duty or taxes. Title to all issues transfers FOB our shipping point, freight prepaid. We will endeavour to fulfil claims for missing or damaged copies within six months of publication, within our reasonable discretion and subject to availability.

**Back issues:** Single issues from current and recent volumes are available at the current single issue price from cs-journals@wiley.com.

## Disclaimer

The Publisher and Editors cannot be held responsible for errors or any consequences arising from the use of information contained in this journal; the views and opinions expressed do not necessarily reflect those of the Publisher and Editors, neither does the publication of advertisements constitute any endorsement by the Publisher and Editors of the products advertised.

**Publisher:** NEW DIRECTIONS FOR INSTITUTIONAL RESEARCH is published by Wiley Periodicals, Inc., 350 Main St., Malden, MA 02148-5020.

**Journal Customer Services:** For ordering information, claims and any enquiry concerning your journal subscription please go to www.wileycustomerhelp.com/ask or contact your nearest office.
**Americas:** Email: cs-journals@wiley.com; Tel: +1 781 388 8598 or +1 800 835 6770 (toll free in the USA & Canada).
**Europe, Middle East and Africa:** Email: cs-journals@wiley.com; Tel: +44 (0) 1865 778315.
**Asia Pacific:** Email: cs-journals@wiley.com; Tel: +65 6511 8000.
**Japan:** For Japanese speaking support, Email: cs-japan@wiley.com.
**Visit our Online Customer Help** available in 7 languages at www.wileycustomerhelp.com/ask

**Production Editor:** Poornita Jugran (email: pjugran@wiley.com).

Wiley's Corporate Citizenship initiative seeks to address the environmental, social, economic, and ethical challenges faced in our business and which are important to our diverse stakeholder groups. Since launching the initiative, we have focused on sharing our content with those in need, enhancing community philanthropy, reducing our carbon impact, creating global guidelines and best practices for paper use, establishing a vendor code of ethics, and engaging our colleagues and other stakeholders in our efforts. Follow our progress at www.wiley.com/go/citizenship

View this journal online at wileyonlinelibrary.com/journal/ir

Wiley is a founding member of the UN-backed HINARI, AGORA, and OARE initiatives. They are now collectively known as Research4Life, making online scientific content available free or at nominal cost to researchers in developing countries. Please visit Wiley's Content Access - Corporate Citizenship site: http://www.wiley.com/WileyCDA/Section/id-390082.html

Printed in the USA by The Sheridan Group.

**Address for Editorial Correspondence:** Editor-in chief, John F. Ryan, NEW DIRECTIONS FOR INSTITUTIONAL RESEARCH, Email: jfryan@uvm.edu

## Abstracting and Indexing Services

The Journal is indexed by Academic Search (EBSCO Publishing); Academic Search Alumni Edition (EBSCO Publishing); Academic Search Elite (EBSCO Publishing); Academic Search Premier (EBSCO Publishing); ERA: Educational Research Abstracts Online (T&F); ERIC: Educational Resources Information Center (CSC); Higher Education Abstracts (Claremont Graduate University); Professional Development Collection (EBSCO Publishing).

Cover design: Wiley
Cover Images: © Lava 4 images | Shutterstock

For submission instructions, subscription and all other information visit: wileyonlinelibrary.com/journal/ir

THE ASSOCIATION FOR INSTITUTIONAL RESEARCH (AIR) is the world's largest professional association for institutional researchers. The organization provides educational resources, best practices, and professional development opportunities for more than 4,000 members. Its primary purpose is to support members in the process of collecting, analyzing, and converting data into information that supports decision making in higher education.

# CONTENTS

# EDITORS' NOTES

The passage of the Post-9/11 Veterans Educational Assistance Act of 2008, commonly known as the Post-9/11 G.I. Bill, created a surge in student veteran enrollment at colleges and universities across the United States. This was due to the bill's unprecedented educational benefits for qualifying veterans who served after September 10, 2001: in-state tuition and fees, a housing allowance, a book stipend, and an additional provision for voluntary matching funds agreements between institutions and the U.S. Department of Veterans Affairs (VA) to defray the cost of either out-of-state or private institutions' tuition and fees. In addition, a new provision authorized qualifying servicemembers to transfer their Post-9/11 G.I. Bill benefits to dependents. The bill's passage has also created keen interest by various stakeholders (including but not limited to Congressional committees, veteran advocacy groups, and colleges and universities themselves) in how the billions of federal dollars authorized by the Post-9/11 G.I. Bill are being spent. This has led to increased scrutiny of, and requests for, data and research on student veterans.

However, although student veterans have been part of higher education for many decades, and The Servicemen's Readjustment Act of 1944 (the original G.I. Bill) is well-known as a watershed in higher education history, higher education researchers have not historically focused on them. This means that military-affiliated students (a term encompassing not only student veterans, but active-duty military studying in off-hours and dependents eligible for transferred benefits under the Post-9/11 G.I. Bill) have not historically been the subjects of large-scale postsecondary educational data collections. Further, these students' characteristics have changed as the U.S. military has changed since the first G.I. Bill in 1944. Thus the study of military-affiliated students is unfamiliar terrain for most higher education researchers who do not possess a significant background in military affairs.

With that in mind, this *New Directions in Institutional Research* special volume provides education and suggestions for institutional researchers to approach studying student veterans. As indicated by the historical review in Chapter 1, data on student veterans are scanty. Federal longitudinal data sets in particular—which many education researchers are used to relying on for aggregate student data analysis—are weak on quantitative data for this population. The federal National Postsecondary Student Aid Study (NPSAS) and Beginning Postsecondary Students (BPS) surveys have some student veteran representation within them, but the small sample size of the veteran

NEW DIRECTIONS FOR INSTITUTIONAL RESEARCH, no. 171 © 2017 Wiley Periodicals, Inc.
Published online in Wiley Online Library (wileyonlinelibrary.com) • DOI: 10.1002/ir.20198

population makes statistical analysis beyond basic demographic data impossible (Report and Suggestions from IPEDS Technical Review Panel #36 Collecting Data on Veterans, 2012, p. 3). Although a 2011 IPEDS Technical Review Panel recommended changes to IPEDS data collection to provide basic data on veterans and active-duty servicemembers enrolled at institutions (e.g., number of undergraduates and graduate students enrolled and dollar amounts of either Post-9/11 G.I. Bill funds or active-duty Tuition Assistance funds awarded via the institution), this data collection did not begin until the 2014–2015 and 2015–2016 academic years (Report and Suggestions from IPEDS Technical Review Panel #36 Collecting Data on Veterans, 2012, p. 11). Further, the panel agreed that collecting graduation-rate data on veterans and active-duty service members was not feasible via IPEDS.

The U.S. Department of Veterans Affairs (VA), as the primary agency responsible for transactions related to the Post-9/11 G.I. Bill, has data on benefit usage by veterans and eligible dependents. However, VA's interest in data has historically been more transactional than research oriented, given its function as an agency administering a wide array of benefits for veterans and eligible family members rather than a research agency. It has recently partnered with the Student Veterans of America (SVA) and the National Student Clearinghouse to issue a report exploring postsecondary outcomes of nearly a million student veterans who began using both Montgomery G.I. Bill and Post-9/11 G.I. Bill benefits between 2002 and 2010, focusing on completion rates, time to completion, and degree fields (Cate, 2014). However, this project will not have full results for some time to come.

National nongovernmental surveys (e.g., the Cooperative Institutional Research Program's [CIRP] Freshman Survey and the National Survey of Student Engagement [NSSE]) also have some data on student veterans. However, because the surveys' primary focus is full-time, first-time degree-seeking students (historically not the profile of many student veterans), the data available are also limited. Another limitation of using nongovernmental surveys for data on student veterans is that many student veterans choose to enroll at proprietary institutions, which tend to participate less frequently in nongovernmental surveys. Thus their student populations—including military and veteran students—are not captured as effectively by these surveys.

How, then, should institutional researchers approach studying student veterans other than using their own campus-level data? The following chapters provide guideposts. Chapter 1, as mentioned, offers an overview of the history of student veterans in higher education. Chapter 2, focusing on conceptual models of veterans' college experience as opposed to traditional civilian student models, discusses how they can aid institutional researchers. Chapter 3 delves into the nuances of the phrase student veterans— which is commonly used as an umbrella term for not only actual veteran students, but active-duty servicemembers, National Guard members, Reservists, and family members using transferred educational benefits—and suggests a data collection protocol to tease out the different subpopulations hidden below the surface. Chapter 4 builds on this idea to analyze specifically, with the use of NPSAS data, differences between veterans, active-duty military, National Guard members, and Reservists on factors known to influence postsecondary access and success. Chapter 5 details data sources available to study veterans at proprietary institutions (as mentioned before, a large number of the veterans in higher education). Chapter 6 discusses state-level data issues in veterans education, focusing particularly on Virginia's State Council of Higher Education for Virginia data system.Chapter 7 summarizes key concepts presented and offers recommendations for further research and practice.

Kevin Eagan
Lesley McBain
Kevin C. Jones

## References

Cate, C. A. (2014). *Million records project: Research from Student Veterans of America.* Washington, DC: Student Veterans of America.

U. S. National Center for Education Statistics (NCES). (2012). *Report and suggestions from IPEDS Technical Review Panel #36 Collecting Data on Veterans.* Retrieved from https://edsurveys.rti.org/IPEDS_TRP_DOCS/prod/documents/Report%20and%20Suggestions%20from%20TRP36_final.pdf.

*KEVIN EAGAN is assistant professor in residence, Graduate School of Education and Information Studies; director, Cooperative Institutional Research Program (CIRP); and managing director, Higher Education Research Institute (HERI) at the University of California, Los Angeles.*

*LESLEY MCBAIN is an assistant director of research and policy analysis at the National Association of College and University Business Officers (NACUBO).*

*KEVIN C. JONES, a former Marine, is director of strategic planning and assessment, Office of Institutional Research, Effectiveness, and Planning, at Polk State College.*

NEW DIRECTIONS FOR INSTITUTIONAL RESEARCH • DOI: 10.1002/ir

1

*This chapter provides a historical overview of the relationship between the military and higher education.*

# Student Veterans in Higher Education: A Conversation Six Decades in the Making

*Shane Hammond*

To understand the experience of student veterans in the academy, one must use a historic lens to gain insight into the longstanding, complex relationship between the U.S. military and higher education. Such a lens can help educators recognize similarities and differences between veterans of past wars and service members today. This first chapter provides a historical overview of the relationship between the military and higher education, including its early origins and the educational benefits afforded to veterans through the original G.I. Bill and subsequent iterations following various military conflicts. The chapter continues with an exploration of the impacts of combat and ongoing conversations in higher education about student combat veterans and their perceived needs.

## Early Citizen-Soldiers

Although America's first citizen-soldier regiments, now called the National Guard, were created in 1636 (Doubler & Listman, 2007), little history exists regarding the experience of student veterans in higher education prior to the U.S. Civil War. The relationship between the U.S. military and higher education began with what Abrams (1989) described as almost an "absence of mind," arising from an afterthought stipulation in the Morrill Land-Grant College Act of 1862 that colleges and universities financed under terms of the act must offer military training as part of the curriculum. Even though the main purpose of the Land-Grant Act was to promote agriculture and the mechanical arts (Thelin, 2004), the Civil War was under way, and Congressman Justin Morrill of Vermont saw the need for fostering military skills as the country continued to grow. The state of the country at that time allowed Morrill to persuade his colleagues to insert the stipulation with little debate (Abrams, 1989; Thelin, 2004).

New Directions for Institutional Research, no. 171 © 2017 Wiley Periodicals, Inc.
Published online in Wiley Online Library (wileyonlinelibrary.com) • DOI: 10.1002/ir.20191

For the first half century following the enactment of the Morrill Act, the military training stipulation appears to have had little impact (Abrams, 1989). It was not until the country's entry into global competition and a provision in the National Defense Act (NDA) of 1916 and subsequent NDA of 1920 that a Reserve Officers' Training Corps (ROTC) in civilian colleges and universities was formalized (Abrams, 1989; Doubler & Listman, 2007; Thelin, 2004). The momentum of this program, however, was short-lived, as the United States entered the First World War, stifling the opportunity for growth. It was not until the enactment of the Servicemen's Readjustment Act (1944), following World War II, that the relationship between higher education and student veterans would eventually grow into a major phenomenon (Abrams, 1989), forever changing the landscape of higher education.

## The Servicemen's Readjustment Act of 1944

The Servicemen's Readjustment Act of 1944, historically known as the G.I. Bill, has been described as one of the most far-reaching events in the history of American higher education, given its influence on physical infrastructure, expanded admissions practices, and government investment in entitlement programs (Kiester, 1994). During the period in which the bill was enacted, the societal importance of academic work was emerging in light of the country's military efforts and a new focus on national concerns (Freeland, 1992). Described as being born out of fear of mass unemployment and social unrest after World War II, the G.I. Bill has gained an almost mythical status in the decades since its passing (Field, 2008). It has been often credited with promoting postwar prosperity, expanding the middle class, and democratizing higher education in the United States by making college a viable option for veterans from a diversity of backgrounds (Bound & Turner, 2002; Farrell, 2005; Stringer, 2007).

Title II of the G.I. Bill (P.L. 78–346, 58 Stat. 284m) aimed to provide support to veterans for education and vocational training through subsidized tuition and books as well as living expenses. Creators of the legislation sought to "replenish the nation's human capital" (Serow, 2004, p. 483) depleted by the decline in college enrollments during the war and the hundreds of thousands of combat deaths and disabilities (Bennett, 1996; Olson, 1974; Serow, 2004). One consequence of this legislation was to push out civilian women who had enrolled in college to open up capacity for the increased demand among male veterans (Altschuler & Blumin, 2009). Initial governmental projections of veterans enrolling in colleges and universities drastically underestimated actual enrollments (Olson, 1974). By the fall of 1945, 88,000 veterans had applied and been accepted for participation under the G.I. Bill (Bound & Turner, 2002; Olson, 1974). In total, over 2.2 million veterans, or one in every eight returning soldiers, attended college under the G.I. Bill (Olson, 1974). Subsequently, colleges and universities experienced a doubling of enrollments. Prior to 1945, student enrollments across the system of higher education had been in decline because of the military draft (Bennett, 1996; Serow, 2004; Thelin, 2004).

Despite scholarly debate regarding the broader impact on the economy following its enactment, the G.I. Bill has been described as innovative at the federal level and as a visionary federal policy, similar to the Northwest Ordinance of 1789 and the Homestead and Morrill Acts of 1862. Each of these policies recognized that, for a nation to prosper, its individual citizens must also prosper (Hyman, 1986; Serow, 2004). Symbolically, the G.I. Bill has been widely accepted as an important moment for higher education, partly representing a transition from a period when college was reserved largely for the elites to an era of increased access and affordability in higher education (Bennett, 1996; Clark, 1998; Serow, 2004).

## The Servicemen's Readjustment Act of 1952

The World War II G.I. Bill helped to shape future iterations of the original legislation, including The Servicemen's Readjustment Act of 1952, also known as Public Law 550 or, more commonly, the Korean War G.I. Bill (Olson, 1974; Steele, Salcedo, & Coley, 2010). Less than 1 month after the start of the Korean conflict, John Rankin, Chair of the House Committee on Veterans' Affairs, introduced legislation to extend benefits of the 1944 G.I. Bill to veterans of the Korean conflict (Bound & Turner, 2002; Olson, 1974). Two years later, the law was approved by overwhelming majority in the Senate and applied to those veterans who served between June 1950 and January 1955 (Olson, 1974).

Although certain provisions of the Korean War G.I. Bill paralleled the original G.I. Bill of 1944, there were distinct modifications to its education and training benefits (Cohen, Warner, & Segal, 1995; Olson, 1974; Teachman, 2005). There are several reasons for the differences between the Korean War G.I. Bill and the original G.I. Bill legislation. Olson (1974) said, "The prosperity and veteran contentment of the postwar years had frightened away the ghosts of the 1930s who had haunted those responsible for the 1944 G.I. Bill" (p. 106). Changed economic conditions had altered the underpinnings of the 1952 Act. No longer was there a fear of a widespread recession or social unrest with the return of Korean War veterans as there was at the time of the original G.I. Bill (Bennett, 1996; Bound & Turner, 2002; Olson, 1974; Serow, 2004). Congress called for a review of the G.I. Bill and other educational programs.

The House Select Committee to Investigate Educational Programs under the G.I. Bill, also known as the Teague Committee for its head Olin E. Teague, proved to be one of the most influential in all of the investigations and hearings surrounding the evaluation of the educational programs (Olson, 1974) and subsequent recommendations for revision to the original legislation.

NEW DIRECTIONS FOR INSTITUTIONAL RESEARCH • DOI: 10.1002/ir

In its final report (U.S. Cong., 2d sess., 1952), the Teague Committee sealed the fate of the educational benefits package in the Korean War G.I. Bill by suggesting the level of assistance provided in the original bill encouraged many veterans to go to school more for the subsistence payments rather than for a primary interest in education (Olson, 1974).

By 1958, there were approximately 400,000 veterans in higher education, representing just 15% of all students, at a time when college enrollment growth began to accelerate (Kim & Rury, 2007). Kim and Rury (2007, p. 306) said veterans had "ceased to be a factor in enrollments," laying the groundwork for further reduction in educational benefits in what would later become the Veterans' Readjustment Benefits Act of 1966.

## The Veterans' Readjustment Benefits Act of 1966

On March 3, 1966, Congress passed the Veterans' Readjustment Act, also known as the Vietnam G.I. Bill (Olson, 1974; Steele et al., 2010). Funds from the G.I. Bill had been unavailable from 1955 to 1965, so for the first time, benefits of the G.I. Bill were awarded retroactively to veterans who had served during peacetime (MacLean, 2005). As written, the proposed legislation covered the Vietnam-era veteran whose service occurred after January 31, 1955, and, reflecting the conditions of society at the time, recommended even fewer benefits for veterans of the Vietnam conflict (Cohen et al., 1995; Olson, 1974; Teachman, 2005; Teachman & Call, 1996).

Unlike World War II and Korean War veterans, Vietnam-era veterans were at a disadvantage in obtaining higher education compared to their non-veteran counterparts (Teachman, 2005; Teachman & Call, 1996). The value of civilian education benefit programs expanded to make them on par or better than those associated with military service (Cohen et al., 1995; Teachman & Call, 1996). Consequently, while veterans of the Vietnam era obtained more education than veterans of World War II or Korea, they could not keep pace with the educational attainment of nonveterans, leading to an ultimate deficit in years of schooling for Vietnam veterans (Teachman, 2005; Teachman & Call, 1996). Cohen et al. (1995) speculate that lower pay during the Vietnam era would have also made obtaining an education difficult for returning soldiers, further widening the gap between the educational attainment of Vietnam veterans and their counterparts of World War II and Korea. It would be more than 10 years after the bill was signed before any further modifications to the G.I. Bill of 1966 would occur.

## Veterans Educational Assistance Program of 1977 and the Montgomery G.I. Bill of 1984

Benefits under the Veterans' Readjustment Act of 1966 were discontinued in 1976 (Cohen et al., 1995; Gilroy, Phillips, & Blair, 1990). In 1977, the G.I. Bill was replaced by the Veterans' Educational Assistance Program (VEAP).

NEW DIRECTIONS FOR INSTITUTIONAL RESEARCH • DOI: 10.1002/ir

VEAP, yet again, offered fewer benefits to veterans than its predecessor. The imbalance in educational benefits and rising tuition costs outpaced the amount of benefits afforded to those relying solely on those benefits to finance their education, limiting access to colleges and universities for many veterans. It was not until 1981 that the U.S. Army supplemented VEAP benefits with the Army College Fund (Cohen et al., 1995). Nicknamed "Ultra VEAP," this supplement offered extra benefits up to $12,000 to selected personnel, but to qualify one had to be a high school graduate and score a 50 or above on the Armed Forces Qualification Test (Cohen et al., 1995). In 1984, Mississippi Congressman Gillespie Montgomery reintroduced an expanded G.I. Bill offering educational benefits to almost all active-duty service members (Stringer, 2007; U.S. Department of Veterans Affairs, 2011).

Gaps in the Montgomery G.I. Bill did not account for the hundreds of thousands of National Guard and Reserve troops who would be deployed overseas during contemporary conflicts. Combat tours of duty lasting over a year left some military personnel with little or no educational benefits (Marklein, 2007; Steele et al., 2010; Stringer, 2007). Military forces serving in Operation Iraqi Freedom (OIF) in Iraq and Operation Enduring Freedom (OEF) in Afghanistan increasingly include a large percentage of activated National Guard and Reserve units from around the country (Rumann & Hamrick, 2010). Conflicts in Afghanistan and Iraq have put the National Guard and Reserves, America's earliest citizen-soldiers, at risk of not completing their college education as planned. Therefore, the passage of the Post-9/11 Veterans Educational Assistance Act of 2008 could be considered a "just-in-time" overhaul of the G.I. Bill at a time when America and its citizen-soldiers needed it most. The provisions of the bill signal another sociopolitical shift, capturing the spirit of the original legislation as written by Congress in 1944.

## The Post-9/11 Veterans Educational Assistance Act of 2008

In 2005, Congress authorized the first update to the Montgomery G.I. Bill since 1984. Called the Reserve Educational Assistance Program (REAP) (U.S. Department of Veterans Affairs, 2010), this program ensured that Reservists called to active duty after September 11, 2001 receive Montgomery G.I. Bill benefits similar to those of other active-duty service members (Steele et al., 2010). Although the Montgomery Bill and REAP helped defray the cost of tuition and related expenses for student veterans, the benefit level was far from sufficient to cover full-time tuition and living expenses at some public institutions and most private universities (Yeung, Pint, & Williams, 2009).

The Post-9/11 Veterans Educational Assistance Act was passed in 2008 (P. L. 110–252, H.R. 2642). This new law expanded benefits available to OEF and OIF veterans by paying tuition and fees on the student's behalf and providing a monthly living allowance and annual book stipend directly to the student (Steele et al., 2010). Much like the original G.I. Bill, recipients of Post-9/11 benefits have their tuition and fees paid directly to the institution.

The enactment of the Post-9/11 Veterans Educational Assistance Act of 2008 marked an important renewal of America's commitment to U.S. service members and, in the spirit of the original bill, rewarded veterans for their "service and sacrifice" to the country (Serow, 2004; Steele et al., 2010). A year after the Post-9/11 Bill was enacted on August 1, 2009, more than 500,000 current and former service members had applied for benefits, and just over 300,000 had used their benefits to enroll in higher education (Steele et al., 2010). Two million returning service members from Iraq and Afghanistan are eligible for Post-9/11 G.I. Bill benefits (McBain, Kim, Cook, & Snead, 2012).

## Student Veterans: Then and Now

Olson (1973) said, "When the G.I. Bill was made into law, no one in their wildest imagination anticipated veterans would attend college in such numbers" (p. 602). Student veterans were different than educators expected (Olson, 1973, 1974). Most faculty welcomed the changes that occurred on campus, but some were skeptical of the veterans and their opinion of education in the early years (Bennett, 1996; Olson, 1973, 1974). James B. Conant, President of Harvard University (1933–1953), found the G.I. Bill "distressing" because he believed it failed to distinguish between those who could be successful in college and those who might be least capable of success among the war generation (Olson, 1973, p. 33). However, despite their early fears of the impact of veterans on the academic community, the majority of faculty were impressed by the commitment and capacity of the veteran population (Bennett, 1996). Veterans were older, more mature, highly motivated, and tended to be better students than the general population (Bennett, 1996; Fredericksen & Schrader, 1951; Garmezy & Crose, 1948; Hadley, 1945; Kinzer, 1946; Kraines, 1945; McDonagh, 1947; Olson, 1974).

Student veterans represented a range of experiences and challenged the traditional practices of college training; thus colleges at the time braced to meet the needs of veterans with an appreciation for their future roles in society (McDonagh, 1947). In addition to changes in academic policy, curriculum, and admission practices, colleges were told to prepare for very real and unique differences between veterans and civilian students given the veterans' combat experiences (Hadley, 1945; Kraines, 1945; Ritchie, 1945; Toven, 1945). Kraines (1945) said, "The veteran who goes to college will present many problems quite different from those of the usual college student" (p. 290). Returning veterans were expected to manifest both physical and psychological symptoms of their combat experience (Hadley, 1945; Kinzer, 1946; Kraines, 1945; Olson, 1973).

The immediate and long-term impacts of war have been long-felt by our nation's veterans, including historical appearances of modern-day post traumatic stress disorder (PTSD). During the American Civil War, a soldier's first experiences with the brutality of combat and war were described as "seeing the elephant" (Grossman, 2009). Later, during the First World War, this condition was described as "shell-shock." In every war of the twentieth century, the chances of becoming a psychiatric casualty for some period as a result of the stress of combat or military life were greater than the chances of being killed by enemy fire, and during World War II it was reported that more than 800,000 men were classified as unfit for military service due to psychiatric reasons (Grossman, 2009).

After the surge of World War II veterans into higher education subsided, veterans began disappearing from college campuses along with most of the special arrangements afforded to them. The composition of students at colleges in the early 1950s began to resemble closely their pre-war selves (Olson, 1973). Herrmann, Raybeck, and Roland (2008) noted after the first G.I. Bill the educational support from the government and the people for veterans continued a downward slide throughout the Korean and Vietnam Wars, in part due to the controversial nature of the wars themselves. Operation Desert Storm, which began in January 1991 and swiftly ended in February 1991, marked the beginning of the Gulf War Era, but prompted few changes to veterans' overall education benefits as a component of the Montgomery G.I. Bill (U.S. Department of Veteran Affairs, 2011).

Current U.S. military operations require more intensive and prolonged use of military power than at any time since Vietnam (Hosek, Kavanagh, & Miller, 2006). Since October 2001, more than two million U.S. troops have been deployed for Operations Enduring Freedom and Iraqi Freedom (OEF/OIF) in Afghanistan and Iraq (Radford, 2009; Steele et al., 2010). Twenty-five percent of veterans separating from the military are expected to enroll in college within 2 years (Hughes, 2011). Not since the Servicemen's Readjustment Act of 1944 have colleges and universities across the country seen such dramatic increases in student veteran enrollments.

Similar to their counterparts from World War II, veterans from OEF and OIF enrolling in higher education tend to be more mature and motivated in their studies than the general student population (Ackerman, Di-Ramio, & Mitchell, 2008; Brown, 2009; Brown & Gross, 2011; Hammond, 2015; Herrmann et al., 2008; Mangan, 2009; Rumann & Hamrick, 2010). This heightened sense of maturity has led some combat veterans to be frustrated with their younger peers and often influence behavioral outbursts of student veterans in the classroom or at the university as a whole (Byman, 2007; Hammond, 2015; O'Herrin, 2011). However, more concerning was a perceived lack of campus support found by first-year combat veterans in comparison to nonveterans (National Survey of Student Engagement, 2010).

Common injuries to deployed OEF and OIF service members include physical injuries such as amputations and traumatic brain injury (TBI) and psychological "hidden" injuries such as post traumatic stress disorder

(PTSD) and depression. Unlike prior wars in U.S. history, combat veterans of current conflicts are surviving and returning to civilian life in unprecedented numbers (Tanielian & Jaycox, 2008). According to the Department of Defense, 85% of injured soldiers in the OEF and OIF conflicts survive their injuries because of improvements in body armor and modern medical evacuation systems. This has led to an increased number of troops returning from combat with PTSD, TBI, or both. These "invisible wounds" of modern warfare can take their toll on the strongest-willed student veterans and present potential obstacles to their success in college (Tanielian & Jaycox, 2008).

Students diagnosed with TBI or PTSD following combat are likely to present unique and unanticipated challenges for faculty, administrators, and staff, as well as themselves (Shackelford, 2009). Greene-Shortridge, Britt, and Castro (2007) found that although many soldiers experience psychological problems related to combat, there is a lag in those who actually seek help for the condition. PTSD, in particular, still carries a stigma that causes many combat soldiers to withhold information that may result in such a diagnosis (Hodge, 2010; Warner, Appenzeller, Mullen, Warner, & Grieger, 2008).

The veterans of OEF and OIF require unique educational and cultural adjustments in order to make a smooth transition from the military to a civilian college environment (Hammond, 2015; McBain, 2008; Rumann & Hamrick, 2010). The influence of the Post-9/11 G.I. Bill's increased benefits will likely have a comparable impact on higher education to the original G.I. Bill of 1944 (Simon, Negrusa, & Warner, 2009; Yeung, Pint, & Williams, 2009). Contemporary conflicts have awakened an important conversation for student veterans. This renewed conversation, stretching across six decades of history, once again calls upon colleges and universities to consider the distinct population student veterans represent in higher education. Further institutional research on this population will help academic leaders better understand the complex attributes of student veterans that have endured both the test of time and societal context.

## References

Abrams, R. M. (1989). The U.S. military and higher education: A brief history. *Annals of the American Academy of Political and Social Science, 502*(1), 15–28. Retrieved from http://www.jstor.org/stable/1046973

Ackerman, R., DiRamio, D., & Mitchell, R. L. (2008). From combat to campus: Voices of student–veterans. *NASPA Journal, 45*(1), 73–102. Retrieved from http://www.naspa.org/pubs/index.cfm

Altschuler, G., & Blumin, S. (2009). *The GI Bill: A new deal for veterans.* Oxford, United Kingdom: Oxford University Press.

Bennett, M. J. (1996). *When dreams came true: The GI Bill and the making of modern America.* Washington, DC: Brassey's.

Bound, J., & Turner, S. (2002). Going to war and going to college: Did World War II and the G.I. Bill increase educational attainment for returning veterans? *Journal of Labor Economics, 20*(4), 784–815.

Brown, E. (2009). Colleges try to ease veterans' move from combat to classroom. *The Washington Post.* Retrieved from http://www.washingtonpost.com/wp-dyn/content/article/2009/09/17/AR2009091704680

Brown, P. A., & Gross, C. (2011). Serving those who have served: Managing veteran and military best practices. *The Journal of Continuing Higher Education, 59*(1), 45–49. doi:10.1080/07377363.2011.544982

Byman, D. (2007). Veterans and colleges have a lot to offer each other. *Chronicle of Higher Education, 54*(16), B5. Retrieved from http://chronicle.com/article/VeteransCollege-Have-a/10596

Clark, D. A. (1998). The two Joes meet. Joe college and Joe veteran: The GI Bill, college education, and postwar American culture. *History of Education Quarterly, 38*(2), 165–189.

Cohen, J., Warner, R. L., & Segal, D. R. (1995). Military service and educational attainment in the all-volunteer force. *Social Science Quarterly, 76*(1), 88–104.

Doubler, M. D., & Listman, J. W., Jr. (2007). *The National Guard: An illustrated history of America's citizen-soldiers.* Dulles, VA: Potomac.

Farrell, E. (2005). G.I. blues. *Chronicle of Higher Education, 51*(36), A31. Retrieved from http://chronicle.com/article/GI-Blues/5396/

Field, K. (2008, July). Cost, convenience drive veterans' college choices. *Chronicle of Higher Education,* pA1. Retrieved from http://chronicle.com.proxygw.wrlc.org/archive

Fredericksen, N., & Schrader, W. B. (1951). *Adjustment to college.* Princeton, NJ: Educational Testing Service.

Freeland, R. (1992). *Academia's golden age: Universities in Massachusetts, 1945–1970.* Oxford, United Kingdom: Oxford University Press.

Garmezy, N., & Crose, J. M. (1948). A comparison of the academic achievement of matched groups of veteran and non-veteran freshmen at the University of Iowa. *The Journal of Educational Research, 41*(7), 547–550.

Gilroy, C., Phillips, R., & Blair, J. (1990). The all-volunteer army: Fifteen years later. *Armed Forces & Society, 16*(3), 329–350.

Greene-Shortridge, T. M., Britt, T. W., & Castro, C. A. (2007). The stigma of mental health problems in the military. *Military Medicine, 172*(2), 157–161.

Grossman, D. A. (2009). *On killing: The psychological cost of learning to kill in war and society.* New York, NY: Back Bay Books.

Hadley, L. S. (1945). Scholastic adjustment problems of the returning veterans. *Educational Research Bulletin, 24*(4), 87–92, 112.

Hammond, S. (2015). Complex perceptions of identity: The experiences of combat veterans in community college. *Community College Journal of Research and Practice.* doi: 10.1080/10668926.2015.1017891

Herrmann, D., Raybeck, D., & Roland, W. (2008). College is for veterans too. *Chronicle of Higher Education, 55*(13), A99. Retrieved from http://chronicle.com.proxy.gw.wrlc.org/article/College-Is-for-Veterans-Too/31872/

Hodge, C. (2010). *Once a warrior always a warrior: Navigating the transition from combat to home.* Guilford, CT: Globe Pequot.

Hosek, J., Kavanagh, J., & Miller, L. (2006). *How deployments affect service members.* Santa Monica, CA: Rand.

Hughes, T. (2011, April 11). Vets go from combat to campus. *USA Today.* Retrieved from http://www.usatoday.com/news/education/2011-04-11-college-vets_N.htm

Hyman, H. (1986). *American singularity: The 1787 Northwest Ordinance, the 1862 Homestead and Morrill Acts, and the 1944 G.I. Bill.* Athens: University of Georgia Press.

Kiester, E., Jr. (1994). The G.I. Bill may be the best deal ever made by Uncle Sam. *Smithsonian, 11*, 129–139.

Kim, D., & Rury, J. L. (2007). The changing profile of college access: The Truman commission and enrollment patterns in the postwar era. *History of Education Quarterly, 47*(3), 302–327.

Kinzer, J. R. (1946). The veteran and academic adjustment. *Education Research Bulletin, 25*(1), 8–12.

Kraines, S. H. (1945). The veteran and postwar education. *The Journal of Higher Education, 16*(6), 290–298.

MacLean, A. (2005). Lessons from the cold war: Military service and college education. *Sociology of Education, 78*(3), 250–265.

Mangan, K. (2009). Colleges help veterans advance from combat to campus. *Chronicle of Higher Education.* Retrieved from http://chronicle.com/proxy.gw. wrlc.org/article/Colleges-Help-Veterans-Adva/48846

Marklein, M. B. (2007, July 12). Veterans tuition breaks expand. *USA Today.* Retrieved from: http://www.usatoday.com/news/education/2007-07-10-gi-bill_N.htm

McBain, L. (2008, Summer). When Johnny (or Janelle) comes marching home. *Perspectives,* Washington, DC: American Association of State Colleges and Universities. Retrieved from https://www.aascu.org/WorkArea/DownloadAsset.aspx?id=4996

McBain, L., Kim, Y. M., Cook, B. J., & Snead, K. M. (2012). *From soldier to student II: Assessing campus programs for veterans and service members.* Washington, DC: American Council on Education. Retrieved from https://www.aascu.org/WorkArea/DownloadAsset.aspx?id=5505

McDonagh, E. C. (1947). Veterans challenge higher education. *The Journal of Higher Education, 18*(3), 149–152, 169–170.

National Survey of Student Engagement. (2010). *Annual results.* Bloomington, IN: Indiana University Center for Postsecondary Research.

O'Herrin, E. (2011). Enhancing veteran success in higher education. *Association of American Colleges and Universities, 13*(1). Retrieved from: http://www.aacu.org/peerreview/pr-wi11/prwi11_oherrin

Olson, K. W. (1973). The GI bill and higher education: Success and surprise. *American Quarterly, 25*(5), 596–610.

Olson, K. W. (1974). *The GI Bill, the veterans, and the colleges.* Lexington, KY: University Press of Kentucky.

Radford, A. W. (2009). *Military service members and veterans in higher education: What the new GI bill may mean for postsecondary institutions.* Washington, DC: American Council on Education Center for Policy Analysis and Lifelong Learning.

Ritchie, M. A. F. (1945). Who should counsel the veteran? *The Journal of Higher Education, 16*(7), 364–368.

Rumann, C. B., & Hamrick, F. A. (2010). Student veterans in transition: Reenrolling after war zone deployments. *The Journal of Higher Education, 81*(4), 431–458. doi:10.1353/jhe.0.0103

Serow, R. C. (2004). Policy as a symbol: Title II of the 1944 G.I. bill. *The Review of Higher Education, 27*(4), 481–499. doi:10.1353/rhe.2004.022

Servicemen's Readjustment Act, Pub. L. No. 78–346, 58 Stat. 284m (1944).

Shackelford, A. L. (2009). Documenting the needs of student veterans with disabilities: Intersection roadblocks, solutions, and legal realities. *Journal of Postsecondary Education and Disability, 22*(1), 36–42.

Simon, C. J., Negrusa, S., & Warner, J. T. (2009). Educational benefits and military service: An analysis of enlistment, reenlistment, and veterans' benefit usage 1991–2005. *Economic Inquiry, 48*, 1008–1031. doi:10.1111/j.1465-7295.2009.00233.x

Steele, J. L., Salcedo, N., & Coley, J. (Eds.). (2010). *Service members in school: Military veterans' experiences using the Post-9/11 GI Bill and pursuing postsecondary education.* Washington, DC: American Council on Education.

Stringer, E. (2007). No soldier left behind: Veterans seek college education. *Association of College Unions International.* Retrieved from http://www.acui. org/publications/bulletinarticle.aspx?issue=42&id=3494

Tanielian, T., & Jaycox, L. H. (Eds.). (2008). *Invisible wounds of war: Psychological and cognitive injuries, their consequences, and services to assist recovery.* Santa Monica, CA: Rand.

Teachman, J. D. (2005). Military service in the Vietnam era and educational attainment. *Sociology of Education, 78*(1), 50–68.

Teachman, J. D., & Call, V. R. A. (1996). The effect of military service on educational, occupational, and income attainment. *Social Science Research, 25*(1), 1–31.

Thelin, J. R. (2004). *A history of American higher education.* Baltimore, MD: The Johns Hopkins University Press.

Toven, R. (1945). College counseling for the war veteran. *Journal of Educational Sociology, 18*(6), 331–339.

U.S. Department of Veterans Affairs. (2010). *RCS report.* Washington, DC: U.S. Department of Veterans Affairs.

U.S. Department of Veterans Affairs. (2011). *Gulf War era veterans report: Pre-9/11.* Washington, DC: U.S. Department of Veterans Affairs.

Warner, C. H., Appenzeller, G. N., Mullen, K., Warner, C. M., & Grieger, T. (2008). Solider attitudes toward mental health screening and seeking care upon return from combat. *Military Medicine, 173*(6), 563–569.

Yeung, D., Pint, E. M., & Williams, K. M. (2009). *Impacts of Post-9/11 GI Bill benefit changes for Army active-duty soldiers.* Santa Monica, CA: Rand Corporation.

*SHANE HAMMOND is a member of the graduate faculty at the University of Massachusetts–Amherst and is a demonstrated scholar-practitioner in higher education with diverse experience in student affairs administration and leadership.*

2

*This chapter focuses on conceptual models that may enable institutional researchers and scholars to better study the student veteran experience.*

# Conceptual Models of Student Veteran College Experiences

David Vacchi, Shane Hammond, Aynsley Diamond

Increases in the student veteran population on college campuses since 2005 spurred a new era of scholarly activity and research on this population. The first wave of studies drew important initial attention to veterans while demonstrating that the field needs more salient conceptual models to understand and study the student veteran experience more holistically and evolve from concepts that only address transitions from the military to higher education (Hammond, 2015; Vacchi & Berger, 2014). A new wave of student veteran scholars (e.g., Downs, Hammond, Hullender, Jones, McBain, Minnis, Phillips, Vacchi) aims to explore beyond the area of veteran transitions into higher education and to examine the success of veterans in college from a more holistic perspective. Although these scholars agree that transitions are only the beginning to understanding student veteran success, they challenge the status quo by endorsing a worldview that avoids deficit modeling, not only for student veterans, but for all student populations.

Frequently cited literature on student veterans (e.g., DiRamio, Ackerman, & Mitchell, 2008; Rumann & Hamrick, 2010) connects with traditional models of student retention, such as Tinto's interactionalist theory (Tinto, 1975, 1993), which may be inappropriate given that veterans are nontraditional students. Tinto's theory implies that students must adapt and integrate socially with a campus context in order to avoid departure, which may not be what is happening with student veterans. Tinto's theory, being "near paradigmatic" (Braxton et al., 2013), struggles with psychometrically valid measures for his constructs (Smart, 2005); it is arguably most appropriate for traditional students (Berger, 2000) and of less value for exploring nontraditional student experiences in higher education, such as veterans. The nontraditional student retention model developed by Bean and Metzner (1985), which evolved from Tinto's theory, has been successfully validated at the model level by further empirical research by Cabrera,

NEW DIRECTIONS FOR INSTITUTIONAL RESEARCH, no. 171 © 2017 Wiley Periodicals, Inc.
Published online in Wiley Online Library (wileyonlinelibrary.com) • DOI: 10.1002/ir.20192

23

Nora, and Castañeda (1993) and Chartrand (1992). Further, the Bean and Metzner model (1985) contrasts with Tinto's theory in the requirement to adapt to a college campus context for nontraditional and commuter population success. In fact, Berger and Braxton (1998) assert, "strong support does not exist across single-institutional studies [i.e., the study upon which Tinto's theory is based] for including academic integration in a logically constructed, internally consistent model of persistence" (p. 104). One of the greatest shortcomings of the recent literature on student veterans is the prescriptive and linear nature of the Tinto- and Schlossberg-based models, which suggest that all veterans should undertake a homogenous academic experience, or process, in order to succeed in college. Therefore, emerging student veteran research avoids homogenizing the unique college experiences of student veterans (both combat and noncombat) and other military-connected students who are (as Chapter 4 discusses) invisible in current data.

Contemporary researchers investigating student veterans in higher education since 2008 have made important scholarly contributions, following in the footsteps of groundbreaking student development theorists such as Erikson (1959), Chickering (1969), Bean & Metzner (1985), and Weidman (1989). Yet the body of contemporary research related to student veterans is still in its infancy. The theoretical models utilized or developed to understand the experience of student veterans from 2008 to 2011 (i.e., DiRamio et al., 2008; Livingston, Havice, Cawthon, & Fleming, 2011; Rumann & Hamrick, 2010) are like an unfinished scaffold, or fluid collection of ideas, built upon prior research and testing prior empirical and theoretical assumptions. Emerging scholars, such as Diamond, Hammond, Jones, Minnis, Phillips, and Vacchi, are continuing to build upon this work to improve our understanding of the experiences of veterans in higher education. This chapter endeavors to problematize the conceptualization and orientation of scholarship on student veterans since 2008 and offer fresh concepts and models to assist researchers and guide programmatic efforts on behalf of this unique student population. After a critique of the literature, three conceptual models offering new perspectives on student veterans will be explained in detail.

## Shortcomings of Linear (Prescriptive) Models

DiRamio et al. (2008) were first to introduce Schlossberg's theory of adult transitions (Schlossberg, 1981) to provide insight into the potential short- and long-term effects of a student veteran's transition from the military to the college classroom. Schlossberg (1981) built her original theory on the prior research of other scholars, including Erikson (1959) and Chickering (1969), out of what she saw as a need for a framework that would "facilitate an understanding of adults in transition and lead them to the help they needed to cope with the ordinary and extraordinary process of

NEW DIRECTIONS FOR INSTITUTIONAL RESEARCH • DOI: 10.1002/ir

living" (Chickering & Reisser, 1993, p. 108). Schlossberg's theory (Schlossberg, 1981) essentially suggests that transitions, midcareer transitions in her conceptualization, involve three aspects: moving in, moving through, and moving out of a transition experience. DiRamio et al. (2008) provided some early contributions to the larger theoretical understanding of student veterans through his observation that veterans can experience difficulty in transitioning from a combat environment to a campus environment because of the clash of cultures. This study signaled a renewed interest by higher education researchers in the experiences of student veterans in college.

Rumann and Hamrick (2010) chose to study student veterans and their experiences enrolling in college through a lens of adult transitions with use of the work of Goodman, Schlossberg, and Anderson (2006), but also incorporated the 4S Model made popular by Schlossberg (1981) as a conceptual strategy for advising adults in transition and adopted by many college advisers, counselors, and mental health practitioners on campuses nationwide. Rumann and Hamrick (2010) built upon the earlier work of DiRamio et al. (2008), and findings from their study suggested student veterans may indeed be actively processing their military experiences while simultaneously negotiating their own personal identity as part of their college experience. Although it draws on the Jones and McEwen (2000) multiple dimensions of identity model, the Rumann and Hamrick (2010) study did not sufficiently address identity development among student veterans. Subsequent research by Hammond (2015) provides a better theoretical understanding of this population by exploring how combat student veterans experience college and subsequently construct a more complex sense of self as part of their overall transition.

Although many veterans separate from the military and negotiate the transition from the military to the civilian context of a college campus, some student veterans fluctuate between these contexts, as multiple deployments can interrupt a college process multiple times. A grounded theory study by Livingston et al. (2011) aimed to investigate and describe student veterans' navigation of college re-enrollment and build upon the base of growing knowledge on their academic and social experiences. Schlossberg's (1981) theory related to the uncertain and vulnerable nature of transitions and was used for theoretical consistency with the prior studies. The emergent themes and analysis presented in the results of this study provided the first transition model tailored specifically to student veterans. The student veteran academic and social transition model (SVASTM) recognized student veterans as comprising a growing subculture of college students in need of attention (Livingston et al., 2011). Unfortunately, Van Dusen's (2012) attempt to operationalize and test the Livingston et al. (2011) model failed to provide evidence of the validity of the model to conceptualize the transitions of student veterans. With 3 years offering only three conceptual articles on student veterans, the field remained in its infancy and was most notably lacking appropriate scholarship to frame student veterans and connect

NEW DIRECTIONS FOR INSTITUTIONAL RESEARCH • DOI: 10.1002/ir

emerging research in an effective and salient way to the higher education literature.

Perhaps typifying this problem, DiRamio and Jarvis (2011) revisited the application of Schlossberg's 4S Model and Tinto's theory that offered some excellent anecdotal perspectives from numerous higher education scholars. In particular, they offer some discussion and an adaptation of Astin's IEO theory in which they open a discussion about the need to bridge between traditional and nontraditional models in exploring the student veteran experience. In their adaptation of Tinto's theory, in which they add a conceptual phase of academic and social development to Tinto's model, DiRamio and Jarvis struggle to make a compelling argument for the use of Tinto. On one hand, they make a compelling argument for the shortcomings of using Tinto's theory to explore veterans (p. 36), and then continue to develop another adapted model of Tinto's theory in which they fail to acknowledge various incongruities with the theory itself. For example, they highlight that populations that connect comfortably only with like-minded peers are at risk for departure (p. 35), then make an argument for a veteran lounge as a safe space and self-segregated veteran peer relationships, which may only serve to isolate some veterans.

This prior research has relied heavily upon interpretive systems of adult transition such as Schlossberg (1981) and Tinto's (1975) "student departure" to find meaning in their experiences. Although both Schlossberg and Tinto have provided valuable guidance shaping attempts to understand student veterans, these frameworks alone are not enough. What has largely been missing from the student veteran literature are models that view veterans as a unique population with unique needs and strategies for success in college. Specifically these models have used deficit models and traditional student theory, as opposed to nontraditional student theory, to conceptualize the experiences of student veterans in higher education. Transition for many of these students is complex, and the paucity of empirical research on student veterans invites fresher and deeper conceptualization of this topic. Emerging scholarship views veterans from a fresh perspective based on strength models or nontraditional student theory to create a more effective way to understand the experiences of student veterans.

## Hammond's Combat Veteran Conceptual Identity Model (CVCIM)

Identity can be thought of as a set of meanings that define who one is based on individual experiences, what role one holds in society, to which group one belongs, or which characteristics make a person unique (Burke & Stets, 2009). William James (1890) first theorized that people have as many "selves" as we have interactions or experiences with others. We take on many identities over the course of a lifetime, and, at times, these identities could be activated (Burke & Stets, 2009). Kasworm (2005) sheds light on the limited research examining the different attributes of adult undergraduate student identity. Dominant frameworks for past research on student involvement and role identity have not taken into account the complexity of maturation and identities shaped by life experiences of adult learners (Kasworm, 2003; Kasworm, Polson, & Fishback, 2002). Jones and McEwen (2000) developed a conceptual framework offering an overview of relationships among college students' socially constructed identities and a conceptual lens recognizing that each dimension of identity cannot be isolated from the others. Building upon the works of Reynolds and Pope (1991), Deaux (1993), and Jones (1997), this model of multiple dimensions of identity describes the construction of identity and the influences of social context on the negotiation of identity (Abes, Jones, & McEwen, 2007). Specifically, higher education scholars have not effectively accounted for the military or veteran identity of these unique students, leading to blind spots in understanding the unique challenges and success strategies that may assist student veterans in their academic pursuits.

The lack of literature related to student veterans, specifically the study of identity and the unique aspects of contemporary war, requires a new lens by which to view student veterans in higher education today (Hammond, 2015). Rumann and Hamrick (2010) first suggested veterans are continuously renegotiating their own personal identity as they transition from a military environment to college. Hammond (2015) expanded upon this assertion by utilizing Gee's (2000) conceptual identity framework and Hecht's (1993) theoretical frame of identity development. Hammond (2015) found that combat veterans could be seen as students in one context but also may be simultaneously negotiating multiple identity roles of soldier, citizen, or peer as part of their daily college experiences. Environmental factors, interpersonal contexts, and the participants' own evolving sense of self appear to influence their ongoing negotiation of identity as combat veterans, students, and civilians. This apparent negotiation and the intersection of each of the themes with core identity are illustrated in a combat veteran conceptual identity model (CVCIM) developed by Hammond (2015) (see Figure 2.1).

This model explains the ongoing negotiation of identity combat veterans enrolled in college experience after a combat deployment and subsequent military discharge. Unlike the empirical findings by DiRamio et al. (2008), the negotiation of soldier to civilian to student appears to be nonlinear and more fluid in nature, dependent upon the everyday interactions and environment that make up the individual's lived experiences (Hammond, 2015). As with most qualitative research, there was no neat fit of the participant responses to an existing transition or identity model as DiRamio et al. (2008) suggested happened for their participants. Therefore, the CVCIM represents an alternative way of understanding how participants perceive their own identity and how that identity is influenced by external factors and relationships, ultimately shaping their lived experiences. Hammond's

NEW DIRECTIONS FOR INSTITUTIONAL RESEARCH • DOI: 10.1002/ir

**Figure 2.1. Combat veteran conceptual identity model**

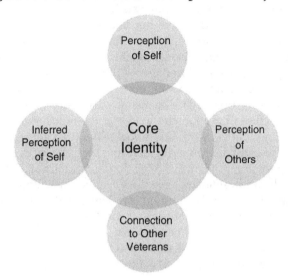

model (2015) includes five unique components intersecting with a primary core identity.

**The Inferred Perception of Self.**   This component results from civilian interactions and illustrates what appears to be a strongly related dynamic tension between a combat veteran's sense of self, created by nonveterans, and the veteran's own perception of self, connected directly to his or her core identity. Despite a veteran's own sense of self-identity, the inferred sense of self can create discomfort or anxiety during their lived experience as college students and results in a selective negotiated identity to help avoid what veterans perceive could be differential treatment by nonveterans. These subtle tensions may present themselves in conversations with other students, in the classroom, or in administrative contexts when working with various student services offices on campus. Hammond (2015) found that these interactions had a significant impact on the student combat veteran experience while enrolled, which may alter a veteran's perceived core identity.

**The Perception of Others.**   This component of the model illustrates how core identity and sense of self are assumed to inform one's perception of others. Combat veterans may see themselves as more mature and more disciplined than their younger peers and consequently believe they have a greater appreciation for their education and the world around them. This perception can translate into frustration in the classroom and on campus that ultimately can lead to persistent distractions and intrusive thoughts, influencing their overall experience as college students.

NEW DIRECTIONS FOR INSTITUTIONAL RESEARCH • DOI: 10.1002/ir

**The Connections to Other Veterans.**   This component explains the camaraderie that combat veterans feel with other veterans and the significant influence this connection has on their perceived sense of self and ongoing identity negotiation as college students. The presence of other veterans on campus and in the classroom creates a cohesive learning environment by providing the support, encouragement, and a comfort level that combat veterans recall from their experiences in the military and during combat deployments.

Overall, the CVCIM provides a model for understanding the complexity of identity for combat veterans and the resulting influence on their experiences as college students. The model further underscores the challenges facing combat veterans in college long after their apparent transition from the military to civilian and then to college student. The process of enrolling at an institution of higher education is but the first step in a complicated experience as these students move through college. The resurgence of this population of students in higher education compels educators and researchers to understand veterans better as complex individuals with multidimensional coconstructed identities.

Taylor (1994) stated that one cannot have an identity without some sort of interpretive system that provides a foundation for recognition of that identity. As part of the next wave of contemporary research related to student veterans in college, Hammond (2015) provides an important building block of empirical evidence related to identity and introduces the CVCIM as a means to focus the theoretical understanding and future research of combat veterans in higher education by considering their experiences through a lens of identity. Vacchi and Berger (2014) first advanced the ecological approach to veterans, demonstrating the complexity with which various actors and agents interact with, and influence, veterans and their identities over time and emphasizing how the student veteran college experience should not be conceptualized as linear. Because transition for student veterans can be viewed as more fluid than linear in nature (Hammond, 2015), the CVCIM represents a way of understanding how veterans perceive their own identity and how that identity is influenced by external factors and relationships. Future testing of the CVCIM will allow for improved understanding of the relationships presented in the components of the model and help refocus the theoretical conversation related to student veterans. Future empirical research on student veterans who have been in combat should consider the utilization of conceptual and theoretical identity frameworks presented here to further the understanding of this student population. This broadened understanding has the potential to inform institutional research and practice for all student veterans. Although the CVCIM emerged from a grounded theory study and has not had subsequent testing, Diamond's Adaptive Military Transition Theory (AMTT) 2012 not only emerged from a grounded theory study, but also emerged from hard statistical data in conceptualizing veteran transitions to higher education.

Figure 2.2.  AMTT aggregate model (Diamond, 2012)

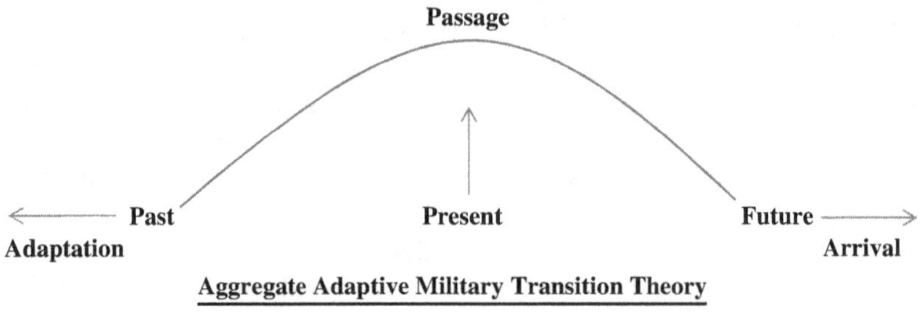

## Diamond's Adaptive Military Transition Theory (AMTT)

An emerging assessment philosophy that can help practitioners assess where veterans are in their transition process from military to civilian life is the AMTT (Diamond, 2012). In observing the prescriptive nature of conceptual models based on Schlossberg's (1981) 4S model as deficit modeling for student veterans, the AMTT evolved from a critical application of Schlossberg's adult transition theory to guide and assess an understanding of veteran transitions (Diamond, 2012). By utilizing this adaptive theory with their veterans, postsecondary practitioners may gain an understanding of how popular static models such as Kohlberg's theory of moral development (1981) may be inappropriate for adaptation to student veterans. At the individual level, the AMTT's aggregate model (see Figure 2.2) represents the path of the student through the transition from military to civilian life.

Four variations of the aggregate model of military student transition emerged from the findings of Diamond's (2012) grounded theory study. These models are examples of the visualization of the emergent constructs identified as Adaptation, Passage, and Arrival. Although each arc is unique to the individual, four arc trajectories recurred among this study's student veteran participants.

Every individual experiences transition at a different rate and intensity, which can vary by incident and occurrence (Schlossberg, 1981, 1984). The adaptive military transition theory is presented as a linear model, because transition from the military is a one-way path with a single destination: joining the civilian community. Represented by a visual model, the slope and length of each arc will change fluidly, dependent on the transition trajectory of each individual. How the individual approaches and progresses through the three phases of transition depicts the degree of transition success. The individual's progression through the *Adaptation, Passage*, and *Arrival* phases is represented by the height of the phase and the length of the arc; the higher the arc, the more intensity and focus spent during that phase. The time the individual spent in each phase is represented by the width of the arc. Throughout the transition experience a unique arc shape emerges as a veteran's transition portrait.

## AMTT Model Phases

**Phase I: Adaptation.**    Adaptation begins the process of military transition to academia. This beginning represents a steep learning curve, as represented in most of the model arcs. Adaptation is usually the most difficult, albeit the shortest, of the transition periods. This phase begins when a veteran decides to attend college and typically lasts through the first semester on campus.

**Phase II: Passage.**    Although the passage stage is easy to reach, it is difficult to end. Passage signifies a comfortable leveling of the transition process. The steep climb from adaptation is over, and this is the time during transition when many participants reported that they suddenly "were okay." Veterans know their routines, have achieved success on first papers and tests, and can anticipate their academic responsibilities for the semester. They also report that, during Passage, they form relationships with other military service members or seek assistance from academic support or counseling services. Veterans make proactive steps to becoming self-reliant and attach to self-selected groups rather than random assignment to orientation groups, for example. The duration of passage can last for numerous semesters, but ideally ends a year prior to graduation so that movement to the arrival stage is achieved in time enough to complete the overall transition before college graduation.

**Phase III: Arrival.**    Arrival can be described as acceptance of the changed life course to becoming a civilian. Participants who are able to articulate their future plans, even if that means their intended occupation or degree, are in the Arrival phase. The ability for a veteran to foresee what comes next is a significant developmental stage in their arrival at reentering the civilian world. The individual agrees to face change once again, this time willingly. Evolving past the Passage phase is a departure from the comfort of known routines, relationships, and expectations—much like Adaptation, yet in reverse, Arrival is visualized as a steep falling off of the arc. The participant at this point is free from the struggle, or climb, into a new identity as a civilian. In Arrival the transition is more of a falling off because of the veteran's ability to acclimate to change from his or her previous experiences.

The AMTT models represent snapshots in time to inform practitioners regarding the adaptation process of individual veterans. The aggregate model in Figure 2.2 is the archetype of the working theory as a visual diagram of a stereotypical transition. Holistically, practitioners can use the four major models of AMTT to understand student veterans' transition rates and intensity better in order to monitor and support effective transitions to civilian society. The following four examples are representations of the model based on exemplar individuals from the study.

NEW DIRECTIONS FOR INSTITUTIONAL RESEARCH • DOI: 10.1002/ir

**Figure 2.3. AMTT symmetrical transition**

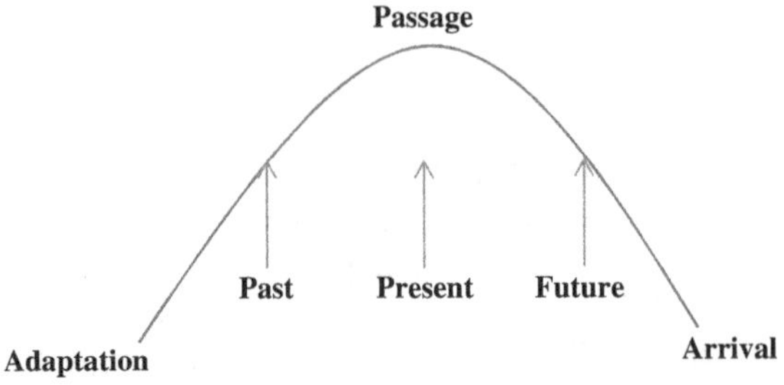

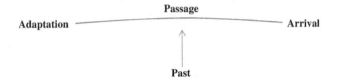

**Figure 2.4. AMTT flat or no transition**

## AMTT Transition Variations (Types)

The symmetrical transition (Figure 2.3) represents a normal transition in which the veteran begins to adapt to a new civilian role before coming to college, and is on track to have an otherwise standard college experience with little conflict or difficulty because Arrival is anticipated. Although symmetrical transition is predominant in the study sample, the individual still experiences each stage of adaptation to their new environment. Symmetrical transition can be used to benchmark the timing and intensity of other transitional stages and as a reference or referral to service members.

Conversely, the flat transition (Figure 2.4) represents the student veteran with whom practitioners should be greatly concerned, as this student is still firmly in a military mindset and has not begun any transition process to the civilian world. Many times this student departed the military abruptly and, in all likelihood, entered college too soon after military service. In all branches of the U.S. military, exit counseling and re-entry training is brief and lacks comprehensive supports both in and time and individual assessment. Although there is an urgency to begin utilizing benefits, correct advising and identification of student needs are paramount to the veteran's success in higher education. Vacchi (2013) noted that some veterans of high intellectual capability struggled in college because their enrollment in college occurred too soon after a combat deployment and they had not returned to their new normal yet.

A stasis transition (Figure 2.5), represented by an arc with no descending trajectory, depicts a veteran who makes an effective transition to college and becomes too comfortable as a college student; thus the veteran will

### Figure 2.5.  AMTT stasis or precipice transition

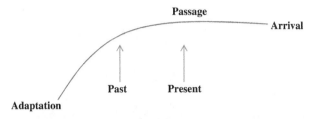

### Figure 2.6.  AMTT variable transition

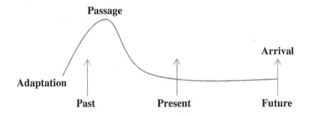

need encouragement to take the initiative to actively engage the process of transitioning out of college and into the civilian job market. This can be a daunting prospect for veterans who lack confidence that their military skills and academic accomplishments will translate into civilian employment. Conversely, the veteran who makes a very rapid transition to being a civilian, as depicted by the variable transition (Figure 2.6), may begin to neglect the important work of being a college student and may need to focus more on their academics to ensure successful academic matriculation. A common mistake would be to confuse the effective symmetrical transition with the variable transition, with the key difference being appropriate levels of focus on the present and performing well academically.

As veteran populations utilize education benefits to pursue higher education, it remains to been seen how prepared colleges and universities are for myriad psychological, physiological, and social needs of their student veterans. At the same time, postsecondary institutions are poised to benefit greatly from the positive attributes this population brings to campus. Many veterans are mature beyond their years as a result of their war experience (Cook & Kim, 2009; Steele, Salcedo, & Coley, 2010). When relating the division between civilian students and veterans, Kim and Cole (2013) state that the differences could potentially reflect veterans' and service members' greater maturity and independence. In addition, noncombat veterans have leadership experiences and have confronted difficult challenges that have matured and perhaps hardened them.

The transition from the military to academia is fraught with change. Environmental, social, and hierarchical differences each require separate adjustment. Experienced together, these psychological, physiological, and

**Figure 2.7.  Vacchi's (2011, 2013) model of student veteran support**

social changes can be overwhelming, even incapacitating, for some individuals. This suggests the need for a more holistic model for student veteran services, such as Vacchi's (2013) model of student veteran support.

## Vacchi's Model of Student Veteran Support

Focusing models on student veterans represents a departure from deficit modeling that can begin to address, insofar as any model can, the unique needs of each veteran. One attempt to demonstrate this approach is Vacchi's model of student veteran support (Vacchi, 2011, 2013). This model adapts theory from several scholars (e.g., Bean & Metzner, 1985; Wiedman, 1989) and represents a broader conceptualization of the experiences of student veterans rather than focusing on a one- or two-semester transition from the military. Vacchi (2011, 2013) developed his model with the use of theory elaboration and considers the student veteran experience from a holistic perspective.

Vacchi's model focuses on the individual student veteran as opposed to a linear institutional paradigm, applies veteran-friendly propositions, and suggests four cornerstones to support the successful degree completion of veterans (Vacchi & Berger, 2014). This model, labeled the model for student veteran support (see Figure 2.7), suggests a vertical axis that conceptualizes the specific and unique services a student veteran may need during transition to and through college. Much of the extant literature focuses on these programs and services, but this literature also leaves a significant knowledge gap in conceptualizing the holistic experiences of student veterans. The model suggests a horizontal axis, drawn from the scholarship of Bean & Metzner (1985) and Weidman (1989), which is likely more significant to the success of student veterans because these areas relate to the academic and social experiences of student veterans while in college.

**Four Key Areas to Support Student Veteran Success.** Emerging and existing research intersect to suggest four key areas in which researchers can explore the impact of college on student veterans (see Figure 2.7). First, services provided to veterans are one of the most frequently discussed areas to help veterans overcome obstacles. In an interview with DiRamio and Jarvis (2011), Alexander Astin asserts that, as with all students, veterans are individuals and have unique needs; therefore, researchers and educational professionals should not seek a cookie-cutter solution to serving veterans. This is sage advice against deficit modeling for student veterans, and Astin's comments recognize the dangers of overgeneralizing about student veterans. However, there are recurring themes in the student veteran literature that suggest several areas in which campuses can be more accommodating for student veterans. Areas identified by Cook and Kim (2009); DiRamio et al. (2008); McBain, Kim, Cook, and Snead (2012); Rumann and Hamrick (2010), among numerous others, include issues with processing G.I. Bill benefits, credit for military service, and disability accommodations in the classroom. Within areas such as this, Weidman's (1989) model suggests that two variables to consider for researching veterans are quality of service and timeliness of service.

A second key area to help student veterans succeed is support to overcome obstacles during the transition to and through college. Some student veteran research does not connect well to existing lines of inquiry despite a robust literature offering myriad college transition connections applicable to all students. Exploring the literature that offers empirical explication for student success or persistence may inform our ability to serve student veterans better than the student departure literature. A study by Pascarella, Terenzini, and Wolfe (1986) on the indirect effects of orientation programming on freshman-year persistence highlights the significance of an effective orientation on persistence and success, a practice that now has universal acceptance on all college campuses. One possible recommendation derived from emerging research is the suggestion that veterans may benefit from a transition course tailored specifically for student veterans (Cook & Kim, 2009). Transition courses can be of great value to the student veteran who is not yet comfortable with the new reality of being a veteran and uncertain about how to engage members of the campus community effectively as a veteran. Another promising recommendation by DiRamio et al. (2008) is the transition coach (p. 93), which is essentially a peer sponsor or mentor to assist a new student veteran in navigating the nuances of a college campus. Researching the effectiveness of transition programming and courses offers a way to measure the success of veterans.

The third key area is academic interactions, which involves frequency and intimacy of contact (in and outside of the classroom) with classroom peers and faculty as variables to consider for research (Weidman, 1989). Contemporary scholars researching student veterans do not emphasize faculty influences on student veterans enough, despite there being abundant evidence in their qualitative data. Still, the emerging student veteran literature considers that ineffective or inconsistent advising and faculty interactions may have a negative impact on student veteran success (Cook & Kim, 2009; DiRamio et al., 2008; Radford, 2010; Rumann & Hamrick, 2010; Vacchi, 2013). Most qualitative research on contemporary student veterans indicates that negative classroom environments are a recurring theme for participants (e.g., Diamond, 2012; DiRamio et al., 2008; Hammond, 2015; Livingston et al., 2011; Rumann & Hamrick, 2010; Vacchi, 2013), suggesting academic interactions are an important key to creating accommodating environments for veterans. The other component of faculty interaction is contact outside the classroom, which students and faculty members tend to agree has a lasting impact on college attendance (Weidman, 1985). If interactions with faculty outside the classroom are sufficient for student veterans or faculty contact is of satisfactory quality, then this may have a positive impact on student veteran persistence. Pascarella (1980) noted the importance of faculty–student dynamics, and the implication for these theoretical and empirical observations is that higher education institutions should implement strategies to ensure that classroom environments are conducive to the success of student veterans. Assessing the campus environment is critical to informing campus leaders about the expected success of veterans.

The fourth key area for supporting student veterans is the effect *personal support* has on student veterans, which has two components. A component of support is peer advising, frequently called peer mentorship, and may not be a function of formal structures such as a student veteran organization or club, or formal peer sponsorship/mentorship programs. Peers can have a strong influence on student persistence and success (Pascarella & Terenzini, 2005; Tinto, 1975; Weidman, 1989) and represent an important pathway for veterans to learn to navigate campuses independently. However, scholars should not overstate the significance of on-campus peer influence for student veterans, as the military culture emphasizes avoiding being the weak link on a team (Institute of Medicine, 2012; Soeters, Winslow, & Weibull, 2006; Tanielian & Jaycox, 2008). Still, providing opportunities for peer support and advice through formal or informal mechanisms for veterans to access voluntarily may be advisable on campuses with enough veterans to support such endeavors. The most important aspect to consider with personal support is that it can, and in many cases will, come from off-campus sources for student veterans.

Failing to acknowledge, or account for, the unique characteristics of student veterans' noncollege reference groups (Weidman, 1989) may hinder efforts by researchers, faculty, staff, and students alike to create an accommodating environment for student veterans on campus by believing veterans are culturally the same as nonveterans. Many members of the campus community know little about student veterans (Radford, 2010), and this may be why veterans report problems with many kinds of interactions on campus, including nonveteran peers, faculty, and staff (Ackerman & DiRamio, 2009). Including the measures *off-campus support sources* and *formal and informal advising* into assessments of the college experience of veterans acknowledges their importance is as critical as academic interactions in understanding the contributors to success of student veterans. Additionally, individuals conducting such assessments should consider measuring both frequency and intimacy of support for these sources of off-campus support and formal and informal advising.

This model connects with the college impact literature through Bean and Metzner's (1985) conceptual model of nontraditional undergraduate student attrition. It deemphasizes the need for veterans to adapt socially to a college context as well as demonstrates that academic interactions with faculty and classroom peers are more important for the success of nontraditional students such as veterans. This framework draws on work dating back to the 1960s (e.g., Spady, 1970; Tinto, 1975; Vreeland & Bidwell, 1966), which emphasized the key role of faculty in the success of students as the institutional representatives with whom students engage most frequently.

The model for student veteran support also connects to the college impact literature through Weidman's (1989) model for undergraduate socialization, which emphasizes the importance of faculty and peer relationships on undergraduate success in college. Although Weidman's model focuses on the social normative contexts of traditional students, the primary relevance of Weidman's model for student veterans is through his suggestion that noncollege reference groups influence socialization outcomes (Vacchi & Berger, 2014). Further, Weidman's model offers numerous logical operationalizations of concepts related to faculty and student interactions that integrate well with measures in the Bean and Metzner model to use for veterans when designing survey instruments and qualitative studies. Specifically, Weidman's (1989) model indicates that if the frequency and intimacy of faculty and peer contact is sufficient in the eyes of the student, then successful college outcomes increase.

## Conclusion

As demographics of college and university students in the United States evolve, so too must the policies and procedures used to assist students in their pursuit of postsecondary education (Radford, 2010). By the passage of educational acts such as the Servicemen's Readjustment Act of 1944 (Public Law 78–346), the 1985 Montgomery G.I. Bill (Public Law 110–252), and now the Post-9/11 G.I. Bill (Public Law 100–48), institutions

NEW DIRECTIONS FOR INSTITUTIONAL RESEARCH • DOI: 10.1002/ir

of higher education have committed themselves not only to educate recently discharged and deactivated veterans and military members, but also to address a student population with unique needs. Student development practitioners must work collaboratively with institutional researchers to adapt strategies to assist the transition process of their military students.

Institutional researchers creating local assessments and scholars tasked with creating large-scale surveys must work to adapt current methods and develop new measures for the success of veterans in college, including the transition from military to civilian life. Advancing student veteran research is necessary to develop a more holistic understanding of this unique population as they depart the military and utilize their education benefits to find a place in the civilian world. The utilization of burgeoning theories such as the combat veteran conceptual identity model (Hammond, 2015), the adaptive military transition theory (Diamond, 2012), and the model for student veteran support (Vacchi, 2011, 2013) can aid practitioners in identifying transitional stages and assigning appropriate support strategies for this most deserving student population.

## References

Abes, E. S., Jones, S. R., & McEwen, M. K. (2007). Reconceptualizing the model of multiple dimensions of identity: The role of meaning-making capacity in the construction of multiple identities. *Journal of College Student Development, 48*(1), 1–22.

Ackerman, R., & DiRamio, D. (Eds.). (2009). Creating a veteran-friendly campus: Strategies for transition and success. *New Directions for Student Services, 126*, Summer 2009.

Bean, J., & Metzner, B. (1985). A conceptual model of nontraditional undergraduate student attrition. *Review of Educational Research, 55*(4), 485–540.

Berger, J. (2000). Optimizing capital, social reproduction, and undergraduate persistence: A sociological perspective. In J. M. Braxton (Ed.), *Rethinking the student departure puzzle*. Nashville, TN: Vanderbilt University Press.

Berger, J. B., & Braxton, J. M. (1998). Revising Tinto's interactionalist theory of student departure through theory elaboration: Examining the role of organizational attributes in the persistence process. *Research in Higher Education, 39*(2), 103–119.

Braxton, J. M., Doyle, W. R., Hartley, H. V., III, Hirschy, A. S., Jones, W. A., & McLendon, M. K. (2013). *Rethinking college student retention*. Hoboken, NJ: John Wiley & Sons.

Burke, P. J., & Stets, J. E. (2009). *Identity theory*. New York, NY: Oxford University Press.

Cabrera, A., Nora, A., & Castañeda, M. (1993). College persistence: Structural equations modeling test of an integrated model of student retention. *The Journal of Higher Education, 64*(2), 123–139.

Chartrand, J. (1992). An empirical test of a model of nontraditional student adjustment. *Journal of Counseling Psychology, 39*(2), 193.

Chickering, A. W., & Reisser, L. (1993). *Education and identity*. San Francisco: Jossey-Bass.

Chickering, A. W. (1969). *Education and identity*. San Francisco, CA: Jossey-Bass.

Cook, B., & Kim, Y. (2009). *From soldier to student: Transition programs for service members on campus*. Washington, DC: ACE, AASCU, NASPA, and NAVPA.

Deaux, K. (1993). Reconstructing social identity. *Personality and Social Psychology Bulletin, 19*, 4–12.

Diamond, A. M. (2012). The adaptive military transition theory: Supporting military students in academic environments. Unpublished dissertation.

DiRamio, D., Ackerman, R., & Mitchell, R. (2008). From combat to campus: Voices of student–veterans. *NASPA Journal, 45*(1), 73–102.

DiRamio, D., & Jarvis, K. (2011). Veterans in higher education: When Johnny and Jane come marching to campus. *ASHE Higher Education Report, 37*(3).

Erikson, E. (1959). Identity and the life cycle. *Psychological Issues Monograph, 1*(1), 1–171.

Gee, J. P. (2000). Identity as an analytical lens for research in education. *Review of Research in Education, 25*(1), 99–125.

Goodman, J., Schlossberg, N. K., & Anderson, J. L. (2006). *Counseling adults in transition: Linking practice with theory* (3rd ed.). New York: Springer.

Hammond, S. (2015). Complex perceptions of identity: The experience of student combat veterans in community college. *Community College Journal of Research and Practice, 40*(2), 146–159.

Hecht, M. L. (1993). 2002—A research odyssey: Toward the development of a communication theory of identity. *Communication Monographs, 60,* 76–81.

Institute of Medicine. (2012). *Treatment for posttraumatic stress disorder in military and veteran populations: Initial assessment.* Washington, DC: The National Academies Press.

James, W. (1890). *Principles of psychology.* New York, NY: Holt, Rinehart, and Winston.

Jones, S. R. (1997). Voices of identity and difference: A qualitative exploration of the multiple dimensions of identity development in women college students. *Journal of College Student Development, 38,* 376–386.

Jones, S. R., & McEwen, M. K. (2000). A conceptual model of multiple dimensions of identity. *Journal of College Student Development, 41*(4), 405–414.

Kasworm, C. (2003, April 21). *What is collegiate involvement for adult undergraduates.* Paper presented at a Symposium of the American Education Research Association, Chicago, IL. ED481228.

Kasworm, C. (2005). Adult student identity in an intergenerational community college classroom. *Adult Educational Quarterly, 56*(1), 3–20.

Kasworm, C., Polson, C., & Fishback, S. (2002). *Responding to adult learners in higher education.* Malabar, FL: Krieger.

Kim, Y. M., & Cole, J. S. (2013). *Student veterans/service members' engagement in college and university life and education.* Washington, DC: American Council on Education (ACE) & National Survey of Student Engagement (NSSE).

Kohlberg, L. (1981). *The philosophy of moral development moral stages and the idea of justice.* Retrieved from http://philpapers.org/rec/KOHTPO-3

Livingston, W., Havice, P., Cawthon, T., & Fleming, D. (2011). Coming home: Student veterans' articulation of college re-enrollment. *Journal of Student Affairs Research and Practice, 48*(3), 315–331. doi:10.2202/1949-6605.6292

McBain, L., Cook, B., Kim, Y., & Snead, K. (2012). *From soldier to student II: Assessing campus programs for veterans and service members.* Washington, DC: ACE, AASCU, NAVPA, and NASPA.

Metz, G. (2004). Challenge and changes to Tinto's persistence theory: A historical review. *Journal of College Student Retention: Research, Theory & Practice, 6*(2), 191–207.

Montgomery GI Bill, Pub. L. No. 110–252 (1985).

Pascarella, E. (1980). Student–faculty informal contact and college outcomes. *Review of Educational Research, 50*(4), 545–595.

Pascarella, E., & Terenzini, P. (2005). *How college affects students: A third decade of research.* Indianapolis, IN: Jossey-Bass.

Pascarella, E., Terenzini, P., & Wolfe, L. (1986). Orientation to college as anticipatory socialization: Indirect effects on freshman year persistence. *Journal of Higher Education*, 57, 155–175.

Post 9/11 GI Bill, Pub. L. 100–48.

Radford, A. (2010). *Service members in school: Military veterans' experiences using the Post-9/11 GI Bill and pursuing postsecondary education.* Santa Monica, CA: RAND.

Reynolds, A. L., & Pope, R. L. (1991). The complexities of diversity: Exploring multiple oppressions. *Journal of Counseling and Development*, 70, 174–180.

Rumann, C. & Hamrick, F. (2010). Student veterans in transition: Re-enrolling after war zone deployments. *The Journal of Higher Education*, 81(4), 431–458.

Schlossberg, N. K. (1984). *Counseling Adults in Transition.* New York: Springer.

Schlossberg, N. (1981). A model for analyzing human adaptation to transitions. *Counseling Psychologist*, 9(2), 2–18.

Servicemen's Readjustment Act, Pub. L. No. 78–346, 58 Stat. 284m (1944).

Smart, J. C. (2005). Attributes of exemplary research manuscripts employing quantitative analyses. *Research in Higher Education*, 46(4), 461–477.

Soeters, J., Winslow, D., & Weibull, A. (2006). Military culture. In C. Giuseppe (Ed.), *Handbook of the sociology of the military.* New York, NY: Springer.

Spady, W. (1970). Dropouts from higher education: An interdisciplinary review and synthesis. *Interchange*, 1, 64–85.

Steele, J., Salcedo, N., & Coley, J. (2010). *Service members in school: Military veterans' experiences using the Post-9/11 GI Bill and pursuing postsecondary education.* Santa Monica, CA: RAND.

Tanielian, T., & Jaycox, L. (Eds.). (2008). *Invisible wounds of war: Psychological and cognitive injuries, their consequences, and services to assist recovery.* Santa Monica, CA: RAND.

Taylor, C. (1994). The politics of recognition. In C. Taylor, K. A. Appiah, S. C. Rockefeller, M. Waltzer, & S. Wolf (Eds.), *Multiculturalism: Examining the politics of recognition* (pp. 25–73). Princeton, NJ: Princeton University Press.

Tinto, V. (1975). Dropout from higher education: A theoretical synthesis of recent research. *The Review of Educational Research*, 45, 89–125.

Tinto, V. (1993). *Leaving college: Rethinking the causes and cures of student attrition* (2nd ed.). Chicago, IL: University of Chicago Press.

Vacchi, D. & Berger, J. (2014). Student veterans in higher education. In M. Paulsen (Ed.), *Higher education: Handbook of theory and research* (Vol. 29). New York, NY: Springer.

Vacchi, D. (2013, April). *Perceptions of veteran-friendliness: Giving student veterans a voice.* Research paper presented at the annual conference of the New England Educational Research Organization (NEERO), Portsmouth, NH.

Vacchi, D. (2011, November). *Who are student veterans and what do they need? Demystifying this special population and framing an approach to understanding the needs of student veterans.* Scholarly paper presented at the annual conference of the Association for the Study of Higher Education (ASHE), Charlotte, NC.

Van Dusen, R. (2012, November). *A study of student veteran persistence.* Research paper presentation at the annual conference of the Association for the Study of Higher Education ASHE, Las Vegas, NV.

Vreeland, R., & Bidwell, C. (1966). Classifying university departments: An approach to the analysis of their effects on undergraduates' values and attitudes. *Sociology of Education*, 39, 237–254.

Weidman, J. (1985, April). *Retention of nontraditional students in postsecondary education.* Symposium presentation at the annual meeting of the American Educational Research Association, Chicago, IL.

Weidman, J. (1989). Undergraduate socialization: A conceptual approach. In J. C. Smart (Ed.), *Higher education: Handbook of theory and research* (Vol. 5). New York, NY: Agathon.

David Vacchi *is the Director of Curriculum Development, Sans Technology Institute.*

Shane Hammond *is a member of the graduate faculty at the University of Massachusetts–Amherst and is a demonstrated scholar–practitioner in higher education with diverse experience in student affairs administration and leadership.*

Aynsley Diamond *is the Director of Faculty Development Programs for the Institute for Teaching & Learning at the University of Connecticut.*

New Directions for Institutional Research • DOI: 10.1002/ir

*This chapter provides a taxonomy of student veterans in the form of a codebook to assist in institutional data collection and analysis.*

3

# Taxonomy of Student Veterans: A Suggested Protocol for Institutional Research Professionals

*Dion D. Daly, Bonnie K. Fox Garrity*

The nature of what it means to be a student veteran has become a complicated and largely misunderstood phenomenon. The phrase *student veteran* may include students who are on active duty, actively drilling as a reservist, those completing active-duty service and transitioning into the next phase of life, those transitioning from active duty following an involuntary mobilization from reserve status and back to lives left behind, or those who are separated/retired from military service. In addition, this term can also include members who reside in the Individual Ready Reserve (IRR), a category of the reserve component that includes former active duty and reserve military personnel who are not obligated to engage in any military activities unless ordered by Presidential Authority (The United States Marine Corps, 2015). Student veterans include those from different branches of the military, who have different intentions at the time of enrollment, use different forms of benefits, and may or may not have a service-related disability. In fact, if an institution identifies veterans as those who are using veteran's aid, dependents, spouses, and survivors of a person with a military background may be included in the category of student veteran. These phenomena may explain, in part, why recent research on student veterans has produced varied results. We contend that thorough identification of the population under study is critical to accurate interpretation of results. In addition, comparisons may be drawn if data have been collected to identify membership in subgroups.

This chapter is grounded in the perspective that differences within groups are as important, if not more important, than the differences between groups. It is based in the idea that students need to be understood in a context of multiple dimensions of identity (Jones & McEwen, 2000). Because many colleges and universities do not collect ample data on student veterans to identify these nuances effectively, this chapter will provide a data

New Directions for Institutional Research, no. 171 © 2017 Wiley Periodicals, Inc.
Published online in Wiley Online Library (wileyonlinelibrary.com) • DOI: 10.1002/ir.20193

collection protocol for the institutional researcher based on a taxonomy of student veterans (TSV). The TSV is presented as a data codebook with a suggested data collection schedule. Use of the TSV will allow the researcher to engage in within-group analysis as well as quantitative research that can account for the potential conditional effects of intersecting categories (Rouhani, 2014). Having a better understanding of the varied groups within the umbrella of the variable *student veteran* may aid the assessment of learning outcomes, the identification of predictors of success, and provide a better overall understanding of how an institution may more precisely match institutional resources to student veterans. (Please also see Chapter 6 for a broader assessment of state-level data collection on student veterans.)

The American Council on Education (2010) recommends that institutions track student veterans by including a question on all admissions forms. The Common Application (used by more than 500 American colleges and universities) asks a question designed to collect students' veteran status, but the question is inadequate, and the available choices are not collectively exhaustive or mutually exclusive. The data codebook in this chapter provides a more inclusive initial question, as well as a set of follow-up questions and collectively exhaustive responses to offer a more comprehensive and accurate method of collection and reporting of student veteran data. In addition, the TSV provides a common method to group and describe research subjects to allow comparisons between findings of various research studies.

## Telling the Story

Although veterans tend to have characteristics in common, they are not a homogeneous group. They exist as subsets within other student groups and as such may hold differing social identities. Categorizing students with the dichotomous variable of "veteran" and "nonveteran" does not allow the institutional researcher to explore the dynamic relationship that can exist between identity and context and may result in spurious results when standard predictors of student success and measures of institutional outcomes are applied.

In addition, the variables included in the TSV are subject to change while the student is in school. If we do not account for these changes, we do not accurately tell the complete story of the student veteran. Therefore, data may need to be collected at various points throughout the student's enrollment.

## The TSV Survey Codebook

This chapter includes the TSV in the form of a data codebook (see Figures 3.1–3.3) to help the institutional researcher uncover the potential in-group variables within the more general student veteran group. For ease of survey

## Figure 3.1. Taxonomy of Student Veterans Codebook, page 1

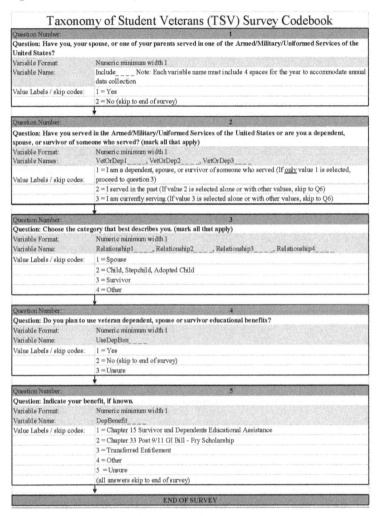

Taxonomy of Student Veterans (TSV) Survey Codebook

| Question Number: | 1 |
|---|---|
| Question: Have you, your spouse, or one of your parents served in one of the Armed/Military/Uniformed Services of the United States? | |
| Variable Format: | Numeric minimum width 1 |
| Variable Name: | Include_ _ _ _ Note: Each variable name must include 4 spaces for the year to accommodate annual data collection |
| Value Labels / skip codes: | 1 = Yes |
| | 2 = No (skip to end of survey) |

| Question Number: | 2 |
|---|---|
| Question: Have you served in the Armed/Military/Uniformed Services of the United States or are you a dependent, spouse, or survivor of someone who served? (mark all that apply) | |
| Variable Format: | Numeric minimum width 1 |
| Variable Names: | VetOrDep1_ _ _ _, VetOrDep2_ _ _ _, VetOrDep3_ _ _ _ |
| | 1 = I am a dependent, spouse, or survivor of someone who served (If only value 1 is selected, |
| Value Labels / skip codes: | proceed to question 3) |
| | 2 = I served in the past (If value 2 is selected alone or with other values, skip to Q6) |
| | 3 = I am currently serving (If value 3 is selected alone or with other values, skip to Q6) |

| Question Number: | 3 |
|---|---|
| Question: Choose the category that best describes you. (mark all that apply) | |
| Variable Format: | Numeric minimum width 1 |
| Variable Name: | Relationship1_ _ _ _, Relationship2_ _ _ _, Relationship3_ _ _ _, Relationship4_ _ _ _ |
| Value Labels / skip codes: | 1 = Spouse |
| | 2 = Child, Stepchild, Adopted Child |
| | 3 = Survivor |
| | 4 = Other |

| Question Number: | 4 |
|---|---|
| Question: Do you plan to use veteran dependent, spouse or survivor educational benefits? | |
| Variable Format: | Numeric minimum width 1 |
| Variable Name: | UseDepBen_ _ _ _ |
| Value Labels / skip codes: | 1 = Yes |
| | 2 = No (skip to end of survey) |
| | 3 = Unsure |

| Question Number: | 5 |
|---|---|
| Question: Indicate your benefit, if known. | |
| Variable Format: | Numeric minimum width 1 |
| Variable Name: | DepBenefit_ _ _ _ |
| Value Labels / skip codes: | 1 = Chapter 15 Survivor and Dependents Educational Assistance |
| | 2 = Chapter 33 Post 9/11 GI Bill - Fry Scholarship |
| | 3 = Transferred Entitlement |
| | 4 = Other |
| | 5 = Unsure |
| | (all answers skip to end of survey) |

END OF SURVEY

creation and data collection, it articulates the questions to ask, the variable format, and a suggested variable name, and lists the value codes and value labels of the responses. In some cases, questions should be omitted based on the response to the previous question. In these cases, skip codes are provided. The goal of the codebook is to provide a ready-made road map that institutional researchers can use in the creation of data collection models within their individualized student data collection systems.

**Questions 1, 2, and 3.** The codebook provides a detailed, systematic protocol for data collection related to student veterans, survivors, spouses, and dependents. The first two questions identify and delineate these groups

NEW DIRECTIONS FOR INSTITUTIONAL RESEARCH • DOI: 10.1002/ir

**Figure 3.2.  Taxonomy of Student Veterans Codebook, page 2**

Taxonomy of Student Veterans (TSV) Survey Codebook (page 2)

| Question Number: | 6 |
|---|---|
| Question: Indicate your most recent branch of service. | |
| Variable Format: | Numeric minimum width 2 |
| Variable Name: | Branch ___ |
| Value Labels / skip codes: | 1 = Army |
| | 2 = Navy |
| | 3 = Air Force |
| | 4 = Marine Corps |
| | 5 = National Guard |
| | 6 = Merchant Marine |
| | 7 = Public Health Service |
| | 8 = Coast Guard |
| | 9 = National Oceanic and Atmospheric Administration Commissioned Officer Corps |
| | 10 = Other |

| Question Number: | 7 |
|---|---|
| Question: Indicate your most recent rank. | |
| Variable Format: | Numeric minimum width 2 |
| Variable Name: | Rank ___ |
| Value Labels / skip codes: | 1 = E1 |
| | 2 = E2 |
| | 3 = E3 |
| | 4 = E4 |
| | 5 = E5 |
| | 6 = E6 |
| | 7 = E7 |
| | 8 = E8 |
| | 9 = E9 |
| | 10 = W1 |
| | 11 = W2 |
| | 12 = W3 |
| | 13 = W4 |
| | 14 = W5 |
| | 15 = O1 |
| | 16 = O2 |
| | 17 = O3 |
| | 18 = O4 |
| | 19 = O5 |
| | 20 = O6 |
| | 21 = O7 |
| | 22 = O8 |
| | 23 = O9 |
| | 24 = O10 |
| | 25 = Other |

(Figure 3.1). There can be, in some instances, a clear distinction between the groups and it is important to collect information on all four groups. The Common Application recognizes the importance of collecting data on veterans and dependents of veterans and creates three distinct groups: those currently serving; those who have previously served; and those who are current dependents (Common Application, 2015). But this question and the corresponding responses do not provide an accurate and comprehensive representation of the student veteran population because the available responses are not mutually exclusive. For example, about 11% of all veterans have spouses who are currently serving or who have previously served (Pew Research Center, 2011). This means that these students reside in more than one category (e.g., currently serving and a dependent or previously served and a dependent).

In addition, the Common Application question does not lead to a set of collectively exhaustive responses. A student that fits the definition of a

**Figure 3.3.  Taxonomy of Student Veterans Codebook, page 3**

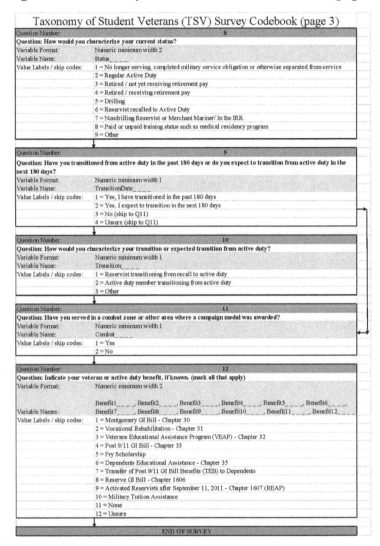

Taxonomy of Student Veterans (TSV) Survey Codebook (page 3)

| Question Number: | 8 |
|---|---|
| Question: How would you characterize your current status? | |
| Variable Format: | Numeric minimum width 2 |
| Variable Name: | Status____ |
| Value Labels / skip codes: | 1 = No longer serving, completed military service obligation or otherwise separated from service |
| | 2 = Regular Active Duty |
| | 3 = Retired / not yet receiving retirement pay |
| | 4 = Retired / receiving retirement pay |
| | 5 = Drilling |
| | 6 = Reservist recalled to Active Duty |
| | 7 = Nondrilling Reservist or Merchant Mariner/ In the IRR |
| | 8 = Paid or unpaid training status such as medical residency program |
| | 9 = Other |

| Question Number: | 9 |
|---|---|
| Question: Have you transitioned from active duty in the past 180 days or do you expect to transition from active duty in the next 180 days? | |
| Variable Format: | Numeric minimum width 1 |
| Variable Name: | TransitionDate____ |
| Value Labels / skip codes: | 1 = Yes, I have transitioned in the past 180 days |
| | 2 = Yes, I expect to transition in the next 180 days |
| | 3 = No (skip to Q11) |
| | 4 = Unsure (skip to Q11) |

| Question Number: | 10 |
|---|---|
| Question: How would you characterize your transition or expected transition from active duty? | |
| Variable Format: | Numeric minimum width 1 |
| Variable Name: | Transition____ |
| Value Labels / skip codes: | 1 = Reservist transitioning from recall to active duty |
| | 2 = Active duty member transitioning from active duty |
| | 3 = Other |

| Question Number: | 11 |
|---|---|
| Question: Have you served in a combat zone or other area where a campaign medal was awarded? | |
| Variable Format: | Numeric minimum width 1 |
| Variable Name: | Combat____ |
| Value Labels / skip codes: | 1 = Yes |
| | 2 = No |

| Question Number: | 12 |
|---|---|
| Question: Indicate your veteran or active duty benefit, if known. (mark all that apply) | |
| Variable Format: | Numeric minimum width 2 |
| | Benefit1____, Benefit2____, Benefit3____, Benefit4____, Benefit5____, Benefit6____, |
| Variable Names: | Benefit7____, Benefit8____, Benefit9____, Benefit10____, Benefit11____, Benefit12____ |
| Value Labels / skip codes: | 1 = Montgomery GI Bill - Chapter 30 |
| | 2 = Vocational Rehabilitation - Chapter 31 |
| | 3 = Veterans Educational Assistance Program (VEAP) - Chapter 32 |
| | 4 = Post 9/11 GI Bill - Chapter 33 |
| | 5 = Fry Scholarship |
| | 6 = Dependents Educational Assistance - Chapter 35 |
| | 7 = Transfer of Post 9/11 GI Bill Benefits (TEB) to Dependents |
| | 8 = Reserve GI Bill - Chapter 1606 |
| | 9 = Activated Reservists after September 11, 2011 - Chapter 1607 (REAP) |
| | 10 = Military Tuition Assistance |
| | 11 = None |
| | 12 = Unsure |

END OF SURVEY

"surviving spouse" is not categorized as a dependent by the U.S. Department of Veterans Affairs (2015a); he or she is categorized as a "survivor" (an option not currently available on the Common Application). On January 1, 2015, the Marine Gunnery Sergeant John David Frye Scholarship was expanded to include educational benefits for surviving spouses. This will result in a growing number of surviving spouses enrolling in college. The TSV addresses these two concerns by providing the following set of responses (mark all that apply): (1) I am a dependent, spouse, or survivor of someone who served; (2) I served in the past; (3) I am currently serving (see Figure 3.1, question 2). All respondents who select only answer (1) are asked to "Choose the category that best describes you (mark all that apply)" and may select among these choices: (1) Spouse; (2) Child, Stepchild, Adopted Child; (3) Survivor; (4) Other (see Figure 3.1, question 3).

There are two additional important elements of the discussion reflected in the first two questions and response sets of the TSV. First, there are a large number of educational benefits (active duty, tuition assistance, service-specific, Guard/Reserve, spouse/family, state) related to military service and many include provisions for spouses, dependents, and survivors. Second, there are those whose service is considered a component of a "Uniformed Service" and not an "Armed Force." Two examples of this are those serving or who have served in the Public Health Service (PHS) or the National Oceanic and Atmospheric Administration Commissioned Officer Corps (NOAA). These two groups may not fit within the historical definition of the term "veteran," but members of each component are eligible for 9/11 G.I. Bill educational benefits (Commissioned Corps of the U.S. Public Health Service, 2015; National Oceanic and Atmospheric Administration Commissioned Officer Corps, 2015). Because the Common Application question only includes "U.S. Armed Forces status," those who are or have served in the PHS or NOAA may not respond affirmatively to this question even though they may have military/veteran aid eligibility. The first two questions of the TSV address these concerns, and are more likely to receive an affirmative response from all potential subgroups of student veterans and/or students not otherwise defined as veteran but receiving G.I. Bill educational benefits.

The TSV can provide actionable data regarding these students. It is not uncommon for student veterans to be confused over their educational benefits (Fusch, 2012). Some of the laws supporting veteran educational benefits have changed dramatically over time. This has resulted in the potential for military members and their spouses/dependents to be unaware of their eligibility. In addition, students who reside in more than one category often cannot use more than one benefit and must make important—and permanent—choices as to which educational benefit will be used (U.S. Department of Veterans Affairs, 2015b). For example, student veterans who are eligible for benefits related to their service (e.g., Montgomery G.I. Bill Active Duty) who are also eligible for the Post-9/11 G.I. Bill as a dependent of an eligible veteran must irrevocably relinquish eligibility for one benefit to receive the other (U.S. Department of Veterans Affairs, 2015b). Student veterans facing such a daunting decision may represent a large segment of the total student veteran group on campuses today, as the Pew Research Center (2011) found that nearly half of all military veterans have a parent who has or is currently serving. Once an IR Office identifies veterans who are also dependents, it can then share this information with appropriate entities on campus such as veteran affairs, financial aid, or student affairs so that resources can be provided to assist the student in making an informed choice, to maximize the educational benefits available, and to provide the best path toward academic success at the institution. Identification of these students should happen during the application process by including question one of the TSV survey on the application form or supplemental forms when universal application forms are used.

**Questions 4 and 5.**    Questions 4 and 5 of the TSV aid in collecting more specific information related to the benefit selection of the student veteran, survivor, spouse, or dependent, in addition to other financial aid data that tend to be collected separately (and typically only from those students who actively receive the benefits). Schools that can identify a group of students who have potential benefit eligibility and who might not be aware of it or who can assist student veterans facing irrevocable educational decisions can better serve those students and positively affect their success rates.

**Question 6.**    Once a student self-identifies as a possible veteran or active-duty military member in question 2 of the TSV survey she/he is directed to question six (Figure 3.2). Because it is not uncommon for veterans to serve in more than one service, question 6 of the TSV survey requests the most recent branch of service. Responses include all of the Uniformed Services: Army; Navy; Air Force; Marine Corps; Coast Guard; Public Health Service; National Oceanic and Atmospheric Administration Commissioned Officer Corps (Navy Military Personnel Manual, 2009), those in the Merchant Marine who have accepted a Navy Commission (U.S. Navy Reserve, 2015), as well as the state forces: National Guard. These groups all share the same defining criteria. Their members hold military rank, are either currently serving on active duty or are subject to involuntary mobilization to active duty, and/or may be eligible for military/veteran educational aid. Institutions and researchers can determine if officers of the PHS and NOAA warrant categorization as student veterans for individual studies, but it is important to collect these data, as these persons may be eligible for military/veteran educational aid.

**Question 7.**    Question 7 collects the most recent rank of the individual. All members who are or have served in one or more of the above listed forces will hold or would have held one of the ranks listed. "E1–E9" identify the enlisted ranks, with E7 and above representing the senior enlisted leadership. "W1–W5" identify the Warrant Officer ranks. Warrant Officer ranks are unique in that only some of the forces use these ranks. Generally, the Warrant Officer ranks include former enlisted members who have become technical experts in their fields and then accepted commissions as warrant officers. "O1–O10" identify the officer ranks, with O6 and above generally considered the senior leadership. Although some differences among student veterans might be assumed based on rank, little is known about the correlation with other in-group or institutional-specific outcome variables. The collection of individual rank provides the opportunity to explore such possible relationships in detail.

New Directions for Institutional Research • DOI: 10.1002/ir

**Questions 8, 9, and 10.**    Questions 8, 9, and 10 of the TSV survey provide greater clarity as to the student veteran's current status and can help an institution better understand the students' transition from active duty. When a student veteran enters or reenters the educational institution, he or she can exist in one of two main groups—those that have a realistic expectation of involuntary mobilization, deployment, and/or geographic relocation at any point in the near future (Group 1: Question 8, answers 2, 5, or 6) and those that do not (Group 2: Question 8, answers 1, 3, 4, 7, 8, and 9).

The possibility of involuntary mobilization, deployment, and/or geographic relocation represents a unique set of variables that must be better understood if an institution desires better predictors of academic success. Student veterans who are on active duty or who are reservists mobilized to active duty may stop-out from school because they have been geographically relocated (e.g., a permanent/temporary change of station, deployment to a war zone, or an individual augmentation). Individual augmentations occur when a military member (active or reserve) receives individual deployment orders that take him/her away from the currently assigned unit/command (Navy Individual Augmentee, 2015). It is important for this information to be shared amongst appropriate entities on campus (such as the Registrar, Institutional Research, and a Faculty Liaison) so that efforts can be made, if necessary, to assist the student in withdrawal from courses (if the event happens mid-semester) and/or to request a leave of absence (so the student can easily return to the school when the event has ended).

In contrast, other student veterans (i.e., Group 2) can be viewed as those who, in general, consider their military days behind them and face no real possibility of an involuntary mobilization, deployment, or geographic location for the rest of their lives. For these students, involuntary mobilization, deployment, and/or geographic relocation are possible but not probable events. These would include enlisted members who have satisfied their most recent enlistment contract as well as the initial 8-year military service obligation, those who are retired, and those residing in the IRR (National Defense, 2011). For these students, an event such as stopping out for a semester may take place for reasons more similar to those of nonveteran students sharing similar demographic characteristics.

Question 9 is asked for the purpose of measuring the timeliness of the student veteran's transition from active duty and can help the institution delineate between those student veterans who have recent military service (i.e., and can be considered in a transition phase) and those that do not. Regardless of current military status (Question 8), all student veterans transitioning from active duty within the past 180 days may have needs that are specific to this subgroup only. Student veterans face unique challenges, particularly within the first 6 months after returning to civilian life, such as rehabilitation appointments, protracted disputes with the medical review board, and physical setbacks (DiRamio & Spires, 2009).

NEW DIRECTIONS FOR INSTITUTIONAL RESEARCH • DOI: 10.1002/ir

In addition, many student veterans face dissonance between their military cultures, work ethics, and value systems and those experienced in civilian life in general (Coll, Oh, Joyce, & Coll, 2009) and in college specifically. Colleges that can identify these students and understand these unique challenges can better support this subgroup of student veterans, so it is important for IR offices to share this information as appropriate. Examples of support include veteran-specific counseling services and an official such as an ombudsman who serves as a student advocate and has information with regard to resources both on and off campus.

Question 10 of the TSV, when used in combination with Questions 8 and 9, specifically addresses the important concept of transition from active duty. The word *transition* (as it is commonly applied in research on student persistence/success) does not share the same definition as when used to describe those students moving off active-duty service, because many student veterans do not really leave active duty behind. Reservists such as those in the National Guard face multiple deployments (Zoroya, 2014) and veterans (79%) have family members who are serving or have served in the military (Pew Research, 2011). For these students, *transitioning* from active duty may not be synonymous with *separating* from military duty/service (unlike transitioning for first-term freshmen being akin to separating from high school). In addition, student veterans who were involuntarily mobilized, deployed, or geographically relocated may alternatively view the time spent away as an interruption of their academic pursuits. As such, the event of coming off active duty may be viewed as a resumption of interrupted studies rather than a transition to a new phase of life. These students may desire to make up for lost time (i.e., increase average credit load), may need remediation in one or more subjects, or may need assistance re-entering programs that operate with a cohort or structured format (e.g., a student who returns in the spring may have to wait until the next fall to resume his or her major coursework). IR offices that are able to share information from the TSV to the appropriate locations on campus can better affect the academic outcomes of these students.

**Questions 11 and 12.** It is well recognized that serving in combat presents different challenges and places these veterans in a different category. Scholarships exist for combat veterans, pension plans make a distinction between time served on active duty and time served in a combat role (Credit for Military Service Rendered During Periods of Military Conflict, 2014), and service in combat can allow admittance into organizations such as the Veterans of Foreign Wars (Veterans of Foreign Wars, 2012). Question 11 will allow for identification of veterans with combat experience, which may help the institution to provide services specific for this group.

Identification of benefits eligibility in question 12, particularly those eligible for more than one program, will allow an institution to provide assistance with benefits access and coordination. As benefits programs continue to evolve and coordination between two or more programs becomes more complicated, it is more important for an institution to provide assistance with this process.

The 12 questions included in the TSV provide a quick and comprehensive method of collecting important military-specific variables to inform both institutional practices and research. The maximum number of questions any respondent would answer is nine and all questions are multiple choice, making the TSV survey a fast data collection tool. Gathering comprehensive data about multiple aspects of a person's service or status as a spouse, dependent, or surviving spouse allows for clarity in the definition of which groups are specifically being included in the term *student veteran* for a particular study. In addition, comparisons between subgroups can be made when the researcher has access to comprehensive information about each subject in the study. More importantly, more meaningful, and perhaps more consistent, results may be found when studies use carefully defined and comparable groups of subjects.

**Data Collection Schedule.**    All institutions may find the greatest benefit from asking about veteran status (e.g., armed service, uniformed service) and/or other military-affiliated groups (e.g., dependent, spouse, survivor) during the application process. The TSV could be included as part of the standard application or initial registration process. Schools with a relatively large student veteran population, that are in close proximity to a military installation, and/or that focus on increased services to student veterans and/or other military-affiliated groups should employ the TSV once a year after the fall semester drop/add period when full-time enrollment numbers are generated (see Table 3.1). Because the TSV begins with a simple "Yes" and "No" response set, the data collected from the TSV will be in direct proportion to the percentage of student veterans and other military-affiliated groups on campus.

For schools with relatively small student veteran and other military-affiliated populations the follow-up administration of the TSV can be included as a step of the rematriculation of a student who has returned from a leave of absence instead of on an annual basis. Those students who leave the school and later reapply for entry would be administered the TSV as part of the regular application and/or registration process. If a student has a military event that results in changes to responses on TSV questions, that event may often require a leave of absence or break in enrollment. Therefore, collecting data upon reentry is suggested for institutions that will not be collecting the TSV data annually.

Unlike variables such as birthdate, SAT score, and high school GPA, the variables in the TSV may not be static throughout a student veteran's college career and any changes can greatly affect an institution's ability to provide services effectively as well as ensure academic persistence. For instance, veteran-specific benefits eligibility can change (for both the student veteran and the military-affiliated student) because of events such as marriage, mobilization to active duty, service in a designated combat zone, and

## Table 3.1.  TSV Data Collection Schedule

| | *TSV data collection schedule* | |
| --- | --- | --- |
| | *Alternative 1* | *Alternative 2* |
| Institutional characteristics | Large active duty or veteran populations OR Online programs offered OR Institutional focus on personalizing veteran services or veteran research | Small active duty or veteran enrollment |
| Initial data collection | All students[a] at time of application or registration | All students[a] at time of application or registration |
| Follow-up TSV administration | All students[a] annually on a consistent date each year | Students returning from leave of absence or a break in enrollment |

[a]Students without a military or veteran affiliation will only answer Question 1.

service at a time or length that qualifies one for transfer of entitlement. The ability for a student veteran or other military-affiliated student to maintain satisfactory academic progress can be impacted by an event such as a spouse being recalled/mobilized/geographically relocated, leaving the other spouse behind to handle family, financial, work, and educational responsibilities on his or her own. In addition, these events can be involuntary, can occur on short notice, and do not always result in the spouse and/or dependents being left behind. Sometimes the spouse and/or dependents accompany the military member (causing a leave of absence or stop-out from the school), particularly when the move is not to a designated war zone.

There may be an increase in support needs such as those associated with death or injury of the student veteran or other military-affiliated student such as a "surviving spouse." Also, it is assumed that the student stops-out from school when an event such as a mobilization occurs, but for student veterans who are taking courses in an online format, this may be an incorrect assumption, as witnessed by the growing number of students taking online courses while in a war zone (McMurray, 2007). Finally, research with regard to in-group and between group interactions on student veterans and other military-affiliated students as provided by the TSV may lead to the discovery of student success factors not yet identified.

The frequency and timing of administration of the TSV is an individual institution decision based on local feasibility and cost-benefit factors, but it is advised that, at a minimum, it be provided at the time of application and after a student returns to the school from a leave of absence. Because

NEW DIRECTIONS FOR INSTITUTIONAL RESEARCH • DOI: 10.1002/ir

changes to student data included in the TSV can represent potential dramatic changes in student benefit eligibility, ability to maintain satisfactory academic progress, support needs, and other related student success factors, it is important for offices of institutional research to share information collected from the TSV with veterans' affairs offices on campus (if they exist) or other offices on campus responsible for student service and retention (e.g., student affairs).

## TSV in Practice

Veterans' stories are nuanced and evolving throughout their time at an institution. Student veterans may transition from active duty, be mobilized/deployed, retire, enter a different branch of service, change rank, or change which chapter of educational benefits they are using. These changes are an important part of accurately telling the story of student veterans and their spouses/dependents and can result in drastic changes in how a student approaches his/her educational pursuits. As an example, those who are facing immediate and involuntary mobilization may approach their lives and their education in a different manner than those who face no such life-altering event. Capturing data on dramatic changes in a student veteran's status will allow for better predictive modeling and more effective resource allocation decisions.

For instance, a student may be mobilized to active duty or deployed to a combat zone while enrolled at the institution. It is generally accepted that when a student stops-out (i.e., does not remain continuously enrolled) from his/her degree program it lowers the probability that student will return and complete the degree (Adelman, 2006). However, there is evidence that this variable may have the opposite predictive quality for some student veterans or their dependents, indicating that stopping-out is correlated with a greater likelihood that the student/dependent will return and complete the degree at a later time (Fox Garrity, 2014).

Historically, research on student persistence has focused on the "transition" of students to college and the necessity that they break away from their past communities (Tinto, 2006). A common theme through this research is the idea that involvement or engagement of the student with the college is essential (Tinto, 2006). If we view students through a filter of "veteran" and "nonveteran" (a between-group analysis) and consider the veteran group as those who transitioned to college after serving in military service (and then left it behind) in similar fashion as nonveteran first-term freshman students left high school behind and transitioned to college, we may make incorrect assumptions of the meaning and intent of a student veteran stop-out. Conversely, when we view this example by way of an in-group analysis, we quickly understand the implied results. Student veterans are not all in the same category as it relates to their current military status, and this status can change while attending school. Some are subject to rapid and involuntary mobilization to active duty, deployment, or geographic relocation, and others, such as retirees, will realistically never again be called to military service (Department of Defense, 1990).

For many student veterans who are mobilized, deployed, and/or relocated the requirement to stop-out is an involuntary action, and as such it should not be considered a proxy measure of individual choice nor should it be a reflection on whether or not the student was sufficiently engaged with the college and his/her educational pursuit. In many instances, the spouses and dependents of veterans can face an overwhelming situation (loss of emotional support, shifting responsibilities, disruption of family roles, financial constraints, dealing with children) in addition to the stress of the loved one being in a life-threatening environment (Marnocha, 2012). An involuntary mobilization, deployment, or geographic location can affect the educational pursuits of the student veteran as well as his/her spouse and may have very little to do with the level of engagement of the student with the school. Institutions that view the event through this more in-depth in-group analysis are then equipped with more specific and accurate information helping to guide their student retention efforts. For example, the school could shift resources away from measures aimed at ensuring continual enrollment of these students and assuming that when these students leave it is a form of failure at the institution. Instead, the institution could adopt measures such as the creation of a separate leave-of-absence policy, making it easier for student veterans/dependents to resume pursuing their academic goals after a mobilization, deployment, or relocation has ended. This can be of particular importance when the event occurs in the middle of a semester. Within this context, the act of stopping out is viewed as a temporary and involuntary disruption of the student veteran's educational pursuits, a perspective that can only be achieved through the collection of more detailed data on this student population.

## Limitations

Use of the TSV will improve an institution's ability to understand and interpret research results. There are two additional variables that might enhance the predictive results but that are not included in the TSV. The first is whether a student veteran has a service-related disability. This variable was not included in the TSV survey because sensitivity to the privacy of medical and psychological information dictates that this information not be gathered and housed in the general information system of an institution. Individual data may be housed within an office on campus charged with providing accommodations and services to all students with disabilities and may be accessible to institutional researchers interested in exploring potential relationships. In addition, data collected on physical and psychological conditions via the TSV survey could result in an unnecessary duplication of data collection efforts based on self-reported data instead of documented and verified student-specific data that are already collected.

A second limitation influences the selection of the dependent variable in modeling student success. It is common for educational research to define success as graduation or retention (continuous enrollment). But the individual agency of the student may result in a different definition of success. Some students may enroll in a few courses to gain skills without the intention of completing an entire degree program. In some cases, a student veteran may enroll in order to receive housing benefits. For many students, the tax-free housing benefit can serve as extra income and may be a motivational factor in college attendance, particularly for those students who have already satisfied their educational pursuits and/or who are not eligible to transfer the benefit to their dependents. For these students, completion of a degree or continuous enrollment may have never been the goal. However, the Courses Precluded; Erroneous, Deceptive, or Misleading Practices Rule (2010) states that VA educational benefits will be paid for a maximum of two terms prior to a student being formally admitted as a degree-seeking student at an institution of higher learning. This is also known as the two-term rule. Consequently, a student who has self-identified as non-degree-seeking while enrolled may jeopardize his or her eligibility to receive veteran's educational benefits. Therefore, while understanding a student's intention or nonintention to graduate would greatly assist predictive modeling of factors related to institutional measures of success, this variable should not be collected by an institution as part of the TSV survey. Researchers engaged in independent studies are encouraged to explore this variable in relation to student "success" without housing these data at the institutional level.

A third limitation is that this survey is voluntary and students may choose whether to provide information or not. To increase the response rate, institutions should carefully time data collection and perhaps consider linking the survey to the standard application or registration process.

## Conclusion

The variables included in the TSV provide a consistent method to describe and compare research related to student veterans, spouses, survivors, and dependents. It provides a system for categorizing and describing research subjects. Rather than the dichotomous veteran or nonveteran categories typically employed as a between-group analysis in research, the inclusion of the more specific variables of the TSV presents the possibility of uncovering additional insight into this varied student population. This then allows for more specific research results and within-group research comparisons. It is anticipated that future research on veteran students will then provide clarity not just between student veterans and nonveterans, but within these groups as well.

NEW DIRECTIONS FOR INSTITUTIONAL RESEARCH • DOI: 10.1002/ir

The ultimate purpose of the TSV is to identify new patterns and predictive variables to understand better the experience and outcomes of subgroups of what are currently studied as one large group of student veterans. If all researchers were to identify their subjects using this protocol, patterns of research results may emerge and better inform decisions regarding allocation of resources to improve the outcomes of all student veterans.

## References

Adelman, C. (2006). *The toolbox revisited: Paths to degree completion from high school through college.* Washington, DC: U.S. Department of Education. Retrieved from http://www.ed.gov/rschstat/research/pubs/toolboxrevisit/index.html

American Council on Education. (2010). *Veteran success jam. Ensuring success for returning veterans.* Retrieved from http://www.acenet.edu/news-room/Pages/Veterans-Jam-2010.aspx

Coll, J. E., Oh, H., Joyce, C., & Coll, L. C. (2009, April). Veterans in higher education: What every advisor may want to know. *The Mentor.* Penn State Division of Undergraduate Studies. Retrieved from http://dus.psu.edu/mentor

Commissioned Corps of the U.S. Public Health Service. (2015). *Salary and benefits.* Retrieved from http://www.usphs.gov/profession/healthservices/healtheducation/compensation.aspx

Common Application. (2015). *Homepage.* Retrieved from https://www.commonapp.org/Login

Courses precluded; erroneous, deceptive, or misleading practices, 38 C.F.R. § 21.4252 (2010).

Credit for Military Service Rendered During Periods of Military Conflict, 20, New York Retirement and Social Security Law § 1000 (2014).

Department of Defense. (1990, March 2). *Management and mobilization of regular and reserve retired military members* (DoD Directive 1352.1). Washington, DC: Author.

DiRamio, D., & Spires, M. (2009). Partnering to assist disabled veterans in transition. *New Directions for Student Services, 126,* 81–88.

Fox Garrity, B. (2014, May). *Individual factors related to student veteran success.* Paper presented at the 2014 Veterans' Summit, Buffalo, NY.

Fusch, D. (2012). *Helping veteran students succeed.* Higher Ed Impact [Electronic Publication]. Retrieved from http://academicimpressions.com

Jones, S. R., & McEwen, M. K. (2000). A conceptual model of multiple dimensions of identity. *Journal of College Student Development, 41*(1), 405–414.

Marnocha, S. (2012, July). *Military wives' transition and coping: Deployment and the return home.* U.S. National Library of Medicine. National Institutes of Health. ISRN Nursing. Retrieved from http://www.ncbi.nlm.nih.gov/pmc/articles/PMC3403397/

McMurray, A. J. (2007). College students, the GI Bill, and the proliferation of online learning: A history of learning and contemporary challenges. *Internet and Higher Education, 10*(2), 143–150.

National Defense, 32, C.F.R. § 1630.2 (2011).

National Oceanic and Atmospheric Administration Commissioned Officer Corps. (2015). *Pay and benefits.* Retrieved from http://www.noaacorps.noaa.gov/recruiting/benefits.html

Naval Military Personnel Manual. (2009, September 25). *Interservice transfer of an officer into the Navy* (MILPERSMAN 1300–082). Millington, TN: Navy Personnel Command.

Navy Individual Augmentee. (2015). *Navy IA frequently asked questions. What is an IA?* Retrieved from http://www.public.navy.mil/ia/Pages/faq.aspx#2

Pew Research Center. (2011, November). *The military–civilian gap: Fewer family connections.* Retrieved from http://www.pewsocialtrends.org/2011/11/23/the-military-civilian-gap-fewer

Rouhani, S. (2014, April). *Intersectionality-informed quantitative research: A primer.* The Institute for Intersectionality Research & Policy, SFU. Retrieved from http://www.sfu.ca/iirp/documents/resources/QuantPrimer_Final_v4.pdf

The United States Marine Corps. (2015). *U.S. Marine Corps forces reserve. Ready. Relevant. Responsive.* Retrieved from http://www.marforres.marines.mil/MajorSubordinate Commands/ForceHeadquartersGroup/MarineCorpsIndividualReserveSupportActivit y/IndividualReadyReserve.aspx

Tinto, V. (2006). Research and practice of student retention: What next? *Journal of College Student Retention, 8*(1), 1–19.

U.S. Department of Veterans Affairs. (2015a). *I am a dependent or survivor.* Retrieved from http://www.va.gov/opa/persona/dependent_survivor.asp

U.S. Department of Veterans Affairs. (2015b). *Education and training: Post-9/11 GI Bill.* Retrieved from http://www.benefits.va.gov/gibill/post911_gibill.asp

U.S. Navy Reserve. (2015). *Navy Reserve merchant marine officers.* Retrieved from http://www.navy-la.com/merchant_marine.html

Veterans of Foreign Wars. (2012). *VFW eligibility information.* Retrieved from http://www.vfw.org/uploadedFiles/VFWorg/Join/sept2012%20ElgibilityFolder2.pdf

Zoroya, G. (2014, March). Study: Recent veterans are succeeding in college. *USA Today.* Retrieved from http://www.usatoday.com/story/news/nation/2014/03/24/veterans-students-graduation-college-completion-rates-va/6735003/

*DION D. DALY is an assistant professor of business and director of external affairs of the Veteran and Military Affiliated Research Center (VMARC) at D'Youville College in Buffalo, NY.*

*BONNIE K. FOX GARRITY is a professor of business and director of internal affairs of the Veteran and Military Affiliated Research Center (VMARC) at D'Youville College in Buffalo, NY.*

4

*This chapter discusses how understanding differences between National Guard members, reservists, active duty personnel, and veterans in higher education can better inform institutional evidence-based decision-making to support military-connected individuals' college access and success.*

# Differences Between Military-Connected Undergraduates: Implications for Institutional Research

*Dani Molina, Andrew Morse*

Since the enactment of the Post-9/11 GI Bill®[1] in 2009, taxpayers have invested more than $53 billion in education benefits to more than 1.4 million service members, veterans, and their dependents (U.S. Department of Veterans Affairs, 2015). Recognizing that the value of a postsecondary credential is a pre-requisite to stability in today's knowledge-based economy, service members and veterans report that U.S. Department of Veterans Affairs (VA) and U.S. Department of Defense (DoD) education benefits are a key factor in their decisions to enlist (DiRamio, Ackerman, & Mitchell, 2008; Eighmey, 2006; Woodruff, Kelty, & Segal, 2006; Zinger & Cohen, 2010). Taxpayers are not the only stakeholders who have made a strong investment in the postsecondary success of military-connected undergraduates. A study by McBain, Kim, Cook, and Snead (2012) found that 62% of institutions across the United States have campus-based resources to support service members and veterans.

The investment made by the public and the higher education community is tempered by evidence suggesting that many with a military service background do not make use of resources and support services on campus. The U.S. Department of Education's (2009) Beginning Postsecondary Student (BPS) Longitudinal Study broadly classifies military-connected undergraduates as "veteran" and indicates, for example, that 44% of these students report never meeting with an academic advisor. Still another 44% report never meeting with faculty outside of class (U.S. Department of Education, 2009). These supportive connections are tied to a student's college retention. Moreover, the literature has yet to show if veterans,

NEW DIRECTIONS FOR INSTITUTIONAL RESEARCH, no. 171 © 2017 Wiley Periodicals, Inc.
Published online in Wiley Online Library (wileyonlinelibrary.com) • DOI: 10.1002/ir.20194

compared to other students with military experience, have a higher or lower likelihood of engaging with campus staff and faculty.

Narratives about military-connected undergraduates—college students on active duty, reservists, National Guard members, veterans, and their dependents—have largely conveyed an attempt to fit these individuals into the success expectations for students at large. Through the *Million Records Project*, Student Veterans of America (SVA) (2014) offers an example of the limitations of a one-size-fits-all success narrative that applies to military-connected undergraduates, particularly those who maintain military service responsibilities while enrolled. For example, the report shows that a majority of G.I. Bill recipients who earn a bachelor's degree take 6 years or more to complete their program. It took 8 years for 74% of G.I. Bill recipients to receive their baccalaureate degrees, indicating that the time-to-completion could vary by their military statuses.

The higher education and stakeholder communities widely use 6-year completion rates as a proxy for student success in baccalaureate degree programs. Using the 6-year time-to-completion window suggested by the U.S. Department of Education for bachelor's degree programs, SVA found that G.I. Bill recipients completed at similar rates as their nonveteran peers (Student Veterans of America, 2014). As suggested by SVA, "it is likely that individuals reporting extended times-to-completion were not continuously enrolled and many factors, both personal and military-related, may have contributed to their longer academic careers" (p. 36). However, questions arise around the required time-to-completion window—do veterans need more time to complete their degrees and should time-to-completion standards change when analyzing this student groups' completion rates? Does time-to-completion vary by military status?

Indeed, a one-size-fits-all understanding of military-connected undergraduates may lead to support systems that overlook substantive differences in needs and characteristics of these students. Worse yet, an inadequately formed understanding of these students may engender deficit thinking that undermines the strengths these students bring to campus. For instance, it is conceivable that veterans who served many years on active duty will take much longer to complete a 4-year degree given their full-time work that lasts several years. By contrast, members of the reserves and National Guard can theoretically begin their college education full-time soon after completing their basic military training, potentially shortening the time it takes them to complete their bachelor's degrees. As a result, campuses might consider developing support systems with these differences in mind.

How do these challenges and issues apply to institutional researchers? As the role and function of institutional research (IR) evolves in an increasingly data-rich environment, higher education professionals will need to leverage these tools to depict a more accurate and compelling picture of the needs, experiences, and outcomes of students on their campus. By broadening classifications beyond *veteran* and exploring how other characteristics may influence these students' college experiences and outcomes, IR professionals can support the postsecondary success of military-connected individuals in new and substantive ways.

This chapter provides new insight into the importance of better understanding differences among military-connected groups. We present descriptive data on factors known to influence college enrollment, persistence, and completion. Moreover, we offer information for classifying military-connected students that will enable institutional researchers to inform campus-wide efforts to build better support systems for these students. (Please also see Chapter 3 for more discussion on specific taxonomy issues.)

## Data and Methods

For this chapter, we analyzed data from the 2011–2012 National Postsecondary Student Aid Study (NPSAS:12), which was provided by the U.S. Department of Education's National Center for Education Statistics (NCES) through restricted use. NPSAS is a comprehensive, nationwide survey of how students finance their postsecondary education. NPSAS also provides a nationally representative sample of students and an effective, cost-efficient way of accurately classifying post-9/11 military-connected undergraduates enrolled at each institutional sector and type (i.e., 4-year, 2-year, public, private, nonprofit, and for-profit). Given that NPSAS is already mandated by Congress to collect and analyze data on America's college students, NPSAS represents a cost-efficient data source to analyze enrollment characteristics and financial aid information among military-connected students. Sponsored by the U.S. Department of Education's National Center for Education Statistics, NPSAS provides important data about the ways in which students finance their college education and also offers limited information about their education and work experiences, educational and career expectations, and demographic information. NPSAS relies on self-reported data from students and also includes data from administrative records.

The purpose of this analysis was to examine whether there were significant and practical differences between the characteristics of students who had an affiliation to the military. Though prior studies have not yet examined points of difference between military-connected students, the importance of these analyses are at least twofold: First, such studies lead to a richer understanding of how service background or responsibilities may influence access, persistence, and/or attainment differently based on military affiliation upon or during enrollment. Second, and because little research has examined differences, this analysis opens new lines of inquiry into the diverse demography of military-connected individuals enrolled in postsecondary education across the United States. These may engender helpful insights about a particular campus' demography of military-affiliated students.

NEW DIRECTIONS FOR INSTITUTIONAL RESEARCH • DOI: 10.1002/ir

**Table 4.1. Number and Percentage Distribution of Undergraduates by Military Status (weighted)**

| Military Status | Number | Percent |
|---|---|---|
| No military service | 21,922,582 | 95.1 |
| National Guard | 31,898 | 0.1 |
| Reserves | 74,310 | 0.3 |
| Active duty | 170,790 | 0.7 |
| Veteran | 855,862 | 3.7 |
| Total | 23,055,442 | 100.0 |

Note: From U.S. Department of Education, National Center for Education Statistics, 2011–12 National Postsecondary Student Aid Study.

**Table 4.2. Summary of Cramer's V Effect Size**

| Categories | Effect size Small | Medium | Large |
|---|---|---|---|
| Two | 0.01 | 0.30 | 0.50 |
| Three | 0.07 | 0.21 | 0.35 |
| Four | 0.06 | 0.17 | 0.29 |

Note: From Field (2009) and Pallant (2010).

Descriptive statistics with the use of chi-square tests of independence and one-way between-group analyses of variance (ANOVA) were performed to test for statistically significant differences between groups. Effect sizes were examined for practical implications. After filtering out nonveterans from the sample, only weighted (WTA000) results from military-connected undergraduates were presented. Table 4.1 shows that there were an estimated 1,132,860 military-connected undergraduates in the 2011–2012 academic year.

Given the large sample of military-connected respondents in NPSAS:12, chi-square and ANOVA tests show that all results were statistically significant (i.e., not likely to have occurred by chance) at the .05 level. As a result, the study relied on examining effect sizes to determine the strength of the relationship between measures of interest and to determine any practical importance to the results. As suggested by Field (2009) and Pallant (2010), Cramer's V is the suggested effect-size measure for chi-square tests and cross-tabulations larger than 2 by 2. To choose a category for reporting, the number of categories in the row and column were individually subtracted by 1. The smallest value of categories were chosen and used as criteria to gauge the effect size.

Table 4.2 includes a summary of Cramer's V effect sizes. Field (2009) and Pallant (2010) also recommend reporting the eta squared value when calculating the effect size for one-way between-group ANOVA. Eta squared

NEW DIRECTIONS FOR INSTITUTIONAL RESEARCH • DOI: 10.1002/ir

**Table 4.3. Distribution of Military-Connected Undergraduates by Demographics**

| | Military status | | | | Effect size[a] |
|---|---|---|---|---|---|
| | National Guard (%) | Reserves (%) | Active duty (%) | Veteran (%) | |
| Gender | | | | | $\varphi c = 0.07$ |
| Female | 33 | 31 | 22 | 21 | |
| Race/ethnicity | | | | | $\varphi c = 0.11$ |
| White | 60 | 53 | 52 | 63 | |
| Black or African American | 11 | 15 | 21 | 17 | |
| Hispanic or Latino | 14 | 18 | 17 | 14 | |
| Asian | 14 | 8 | 2 | 3 | |
| Other or multiracial | 1 | 7 | 8 | 4 | |
| Age upon entry into postsecondary education (average) | 20 | 22 | 22 | 25 | $\eta^2 = 0.03$ |

Note: From U.S. Department of Education, National Center for Education Statistics, 2011–2012 National Postsecondary Student Aid Study (NPSAS:12).
[a]Effect size $\varphi c$ denotes Cramer's V and $\eta^2$ denotes eta squared.

is calculated by dividing the sum of squares between groups by the total sum of squares. An eta squared of .01 suggests a small effect, while eta squared of .06 and .14 suggests a medium and large effect, respectively (Field, 2009; Pallant, 2010). Although a full list of factors examined in this study can be found in Table 4.3, Table 4.2 includes suggested thresholds for classifying small, medium, and large effect sizes based upon the number of categories being considered.

## Findings

**Demographic Characteristics of Military-Connected Undergraduates.** A number of differences were found between military-connected undergraduates on factors related to their demographics and income. Table 4.3 shows that roughly one third of National Guard members (33%) and reservist (31%) undergraduates were female, whereas one in five active-duty members (22%) and veterans (21%) were female.

In terms of race/ethnicity, about half of active-duty members (48%) and reservists (47%) were racial/ethnic minorities, which include Black/African American, Hispanic/Latino, Asian, or multiracial students. A larger share of veterans (63%) and members of the National Guard (60%) identified as White. This is an interesting finding given that veterans typically come from the active-duty ranks. The results showing that a larger percentage of veterans were White may mean that a higher percentage of racial/ethnic minorities remained on the active duty force and more White service members

### Table 4.4. Distribution of Military-Connected Undergraduates by Income

| | Military status | | | | |
| --- | --- | --- | --- | --- | --- |
| | National Guard | Reserves | Active duty | Veteran | Effect size[a] |
| Adjusted gross income (average) | $47,504 | $34,938 | $35,413 | $30,539 | $\eta^2 = .01$ |

Note: From U.S. Department of Education, National Center for Education Statistics, 2011–2012 National Postsecondary Student Aid Study (NPSAS:12).
[a]Effect size $\eta^2$ denotes eta squared.

transitioned out of the active-duty military. However, it is unclear why there was a large percentage of White National Guard college students relative to their active duty and reserve counterparts.

Military-connected undergraduates' age of entry into college was found to differ by service background. Table 4.3 shows the average member of the National Guard first attended college at 20 years of age. By contrast, the average age of veterans at the start of college was 25, roughly 5 years later than their National Guard counterparts. As expected, veterans were shown to wait to enroll in college until after they completed their time on active-duty service. However, it is not clear why reservists waited slightly longer than National Guard members even though they are not full-time military personnel. It may be that reservists were called to active-duty service given the wars in Iraq and Afghanistan, where a large number of reservists were ordered to active-duty service.

Statistically significant differences were found between military-connected undergraduates when examining their income (Table 4.4). For instance, veterans had an average adjusted gross income of $30,539 while National Guard members averaged $47,504 in gross income, a difference of nearly $17,000. Although further research is necessary, it is possible that National Guard members suffered less interruption of employment and thus averaged higher gross incomes.

**Enrollment Characteristics of Military-Connected Undergraduates.** In terms of attendance intensity by military status, Table 4.5 shows that a majority of National Guard members (56%) and, to a slightly lesser extent, veterans (51%) were attending college exclusively full-time. Unsurprisingly, a majority of active-duty members (61%) were in college part-time, likely a result of their full-time active military service. The relationship between attendance intensity and military status is between low to moderate strength (V = 0.15), indicating that there is a low to moderate association between military status and whether a military-connected student went to college part- or full-time, or a mix of both.

When examining the proportion of classes taken completely online, clear differences were found between military-connected students. As

NEW DIRECTIONS FOR INSTITUTIONAL RESEARCH • DOI: 10.1002/ir

**Table 4.5. Distribution of Military-Connected Undergraduates by Enrollment Characteristics**

| | Military status | | | | |
|---|---|---|---|---|---|
| | National Guard (%) | Reserves (%) | Active duty (%) | Veteran (%) | Effect size[a] |
| Attend institution in state of legal residence | | | | | $\varphi c = 0.18$ |
| Yes | 86 | 71 | 45 | 77 | |
| Attendance intensity | | | | | $\varphi c = 0.15$ |
| Exclusively full-time | 56 | 41 | 31 | 51 | |
| Exclusively part-time | 26 | 46 | 61 | 32 | |
| Mixed full-time and part-time | 19 | 13 | 9 | 17 | |
| Proportion of classes taken completely online (only respondents who took alternative courses) | | | | | $\varphi c = 0.22$ |
| All | 28 | 21 | 59 | 22 | |
| Some | 51 | 40 | 21 | 41 | |
| None | 21 | 39 | 20 | 37 | |

Note: From U.S. Department of Education, National Center for Education Statistics, 2011–2012 National Postsecondary Student Aid Study (NPSAS:12).
[a]Effect size $\varphi c$ denotes Cramer's V.

shown in Table 4.5, a majority of active-duty members (59%) who took alternative courses (i.e., evening, weekend, and online) took their courses completely online. By contrast, a smaller share of reservists (39%) and veterans (37%) did not take any of their alternative courses online. In addition to being a statistically significant relationship, the Cramer's V value of 0.22 suggests that the association is between a moderate and large effect. As expected, the full-time employment requirements of active-duty individuals may have limited their likelihood of attending college on campus. As a result, a clear majority (80%) took all or some of their college coursework online. However, it is unclear why more reservists, compared to their National Guard counters, did not take any courses online, even though they were both part of the reserve component of the military. There remain unexamined factors that are influencing alternative coursework choice between the reserve forces.

One of the most notable results in this study was the chi-square analysis of military status and college attendance in state of legal residence. Findings showed that a majority of National Guard members (86%), veterans (77%), and reservists (71%) attended college in their state of legal residence. By contrast, a much smaller share of active-duty members (45%) had enrolled in college in their state of legal residence. The relationship between military

**Table 4.6. Distribution of Military-Connected Undergraduates by Employment**

|  | Military status | | | | |
|---|---|---|---|---|---|
|  | National Guard (%) | Reserves (%) | Active duty (%) | Veteran (%) | Effect size[a] |
| Full-time or part-time job while enrolled in school (excluding work-study) |  |  |  |  | $\varphi c = 0.16$ |
| No job | 24 | 31 | 19 | 37 |  |
| Part-time | 40 | 33 | 11 | 22 |  |
| Full-time | 36 | 36 | 70 | 42 |  |

Note: From U.S. Department of Education, National Center for Education Statistics, 2011–2012 National Postsecondary Student Aid Study (NPSAS:12).
[a]Effect size $\varphi c$ denotes Cramer's V.

status and attendance in state of legal residence was found to be moderate ($V = 0.18$), signaling that the differences have substantive implications. Given that respondents with active-duty status were more likely to report taking classes online, it is not surprising that less than half of respondents on active duty enrolled in an institution in their state of legal residence. Taken together, these findings suggest that active-duty military personnel sought more convenient options for pursuing their undergraduate degrees, which may or may not be as cost-efficient had they enrolled in public institutions within their state of legal residence.

**Employment of Military-Connected Undergraduates.** Among military-connected undergraduates, those who maintained military service obligations while enrolled were more likely to have a full- or part-time job. As shown in Table 4.6, a majority of active-duty members (70%) were full-time employees. Among military-connected students with no job in college, veterans had the largest percentage (37%) not employed while pursuing a college education. A Cramer's V of 0.16 indicated a moderate relationship between employment and military status. Not surprisingly, most students on active duty were employed full-time. However, there are 30% who were not full-time employees, likely a result of participation as a Reserve Officers' Training Corps (ROTC) cadet/NROTC midshipman, Green to Gold program, or release from full-time service to attain an advanced graduate/professional degree among the officer ranks. Moreover, the large share of veterans who had no job while in college showed that many may decide to take up higher education as a full-time position (as found in the enrollment characteristics section of this chapter) once they have completed their length-of-service obligations. However, a large share of veterans (42%) maintained full-time employment status even after their active-duty service, likely a result of family

**Table 4.7.  Distribution of Military-Connected Undergraduates by Financial Aid**

| | Military status | | | | |
|---|---|---|---|---|---|
| | National Guard | Reserves | Active duty | Veteran | Effect size[a] |
| Financial aid | | | | | |
| Applied for any aid (%) | 85 | 89 | 88 | 89 | $\varphi c = 0.03$ |
| Received any aid (%) | 83 | 87 | 81 | 85 | $\varphi c = 0.04$ |
| Received grants (%) | 59 | 57 | 48 | 52 | $\varphi c = 0.05$ |
| Received loans (%) | 27 | 24 | 9 | 31 | $\varphi c = 0.18$ |
| Received VA/DoD benefits (%) | 46 | 68 | 54 | 59 | $\varphi c = 0.08$ |
| Received a refund (%) | 28 | 26 | 13 | 30 | $\varphi c = 0.13$ |
| Average total aid | $6,976 | $8,480 | $4,565 | $9,889 | $\eta^2 = 0.04$ |
| Average total grants | $2,486 | $1,848 | $1,648 | $2,122 | $\eta^2 = 0.00$ |
| Average total loans | $2,344 | $1,580 | $566 | $2,430 | $\eta^2 = 0.03$ |
| Average VA/DoD benefits | $2,087 | $5,020 | $2,331 | $5,247 | $\eta^2 = 0.02$ |

Note: From U.S. Department of Education, National Center for Education Statistics, 2011–2012 National Postsecondary Student Aid Study (NPSAS:12).
[a]Effect size $\varphi c$ denotes Cramer's V and $\eta^2$ denotes eta squared.

responsibilities or the need to sustain a standard of living acquired while on active duty.

**Financial Aid Received by Military-Connected Undergraduates.** The results showed that a majority of military-connected undergraduates who applied for financial aid received such aid, which included federal, state, institutional, and private loans, grants, work-study, and other forms of financial aid. However, notable differences were found by type of aid received and their respective amounts. Table 4.7 illustrates that a large share of National Guard members (59%) and reservists (57%) had received aid in the form of grants, whereas roughly half of veterans (52%) and active-duty members (48%) had received grant aid. When loan recipients were examined more closely, cross-tabulations showed that a minority of military-connected individuals received such aid. The largest distribution of military-connected students who received loans were veterans (31%) and the smallest share were active-duty members (9%), a 22-percentage point difference. Although the Cramer's V effect sizes indicated the existence of low to moderate relationships in financial aid received, the association between military status and loans received had a larger effect size. The findings related to loans received are important to highlight. The higher percentage of veterans who received loans, when compared to their other military-connected counterparts, suggests that leaving the military after active duty may necessitate taking on increased debt to cover the costs of maintaining a standard of living and/or family responsibilities. In contrast, students on active duty were more likely to have their housing and food costs covered by the military. Reservists also had to take on additional debt in college, likely in part due to the fact that their part-time military service limits the amount of educational expenses that can be covered by the military.

Marked differences were also found in college financing by VA/DoD benefits received and military status. Over 65% of reservists received VA/DoD benefits, and 46% of National Guard members received VA/DoD benefits, a difference of 19 percentage points. The large discrepancy in VA/DoD education benefits received could be a result of available education benefits extended to these military-connected groups. It is possible that members of the National Guard relied more on state education benefits than on federal VA/DoD programs to defray college costs. Moreover, they may have been ineligible for VA/DoD education programs given the amount of active-duty time required for VA/DoD benefits. However, it is not clear why only 59% of veterans utilized VA/DoD benefits, even though they were more likely to have a larger time on active-duty service, and consequently, had more VA education benefits available to them. It is possible that reservists were able to use several VA/DoD education programs simultaneously, and as a result, a larger share drew from these benefits to cover their higher education expenses.

Lastly, a minority of military-connected students received a refund of scholarships, grants, or loans; with a larger share of veterans (30%) receiving money in return after paying for tuition and fees. The association between military status and receiving any refund fell between a low to moderate effect size ($V = 0.13$). Remarkably, not a large share of military-connected students received a refund after paying for their tuition and fees, particularly among active-duty undergraduates. The results showed that a large share of reservists and veterans report utilizing financial aid that need not be repaid (i.e., grants and VA/DoD benefits) to cover the costs of higher education. The results were mixed for members of the National Guard and active duty.

**Risk Factors Among Military-Connected Undergraduates.** A focus of this chapter was to examine how several factors discussed above—delaying college enrollment, dependent status, single-parent status, and employment while in college—differ among military-connected students and to examine the potential impact on their college completion. In fact, the U.S. Department of Education and others (Educational Testing Service, 2000; Schmid & Abell, 2003; U.S. Department of Education, 1995, 2002, 2011; 2015) have identified seven factors that may impede college persistence and attainment among nontraditional students. These factors include (a) delayed college enrollment, (b) no high school diploma, (c) part-time college enrollment, (d) financially independent, (e) have dependents, (f) single-parent status, and (g) full-time work while in college (see Table 4.8). Among military-connected undergraduates, chi-square distributions showed that a significant share of active-duty members had four or more of these risk factors while in college (60%). By contrast, 44% of veterans, 37% of reservists,

**Table 4.8. Distribution of Military-Connected Undergraduates by Risk Factors**

| | Military status | | | | |
|---|---|---|---|---|---|
| | National Guard (%) | Reserves (%) | Active duty (%) | Veteran (%) | Effect size[a] |
| Risk index | | | | | $\varphi c = 0.18$ |
| None | 6 | 8 | 0 | 0 | |
| One | 16 | 10 | 4 | 7 | |
| Two | 29 | 14 | 12 | 23 | |
| Three | 19 | 32 | 24 | 26 | |
| Four | 24 | 21 | 32 | 25 | |
| Five | 6 | 13 | 24 | 15 | |
| Six | 1 | 3 | 5 | 3 | |
| Seven | 0 | 0 | 1 | 1 | |

Note: From U.S. Department of Education, National Center for Education Statistics, 2011–2012 National Postsecondary Student Aid Study (NPSAS:12).
[a]Effect size $\varphi c$ denotes Cramer's V.

and 31% of National Guard members had four or more circumstances associated with not completing their higher education. In addition to being a statistically significant relationship, the Cramer's V value of 0.18 suggests that the association is of moderate to large effect, meaning that the relationship between military-connected students and risk of not completing college is of substantive importance.

**Implications for Institutional Researchers.** For decades, institutional researchers have compiled information to guide effective decision making by campus leaders. As data have become increasingly integral to strategic planning priorities and accountability responsibilities, institutional researchers' function has evolved to a more central and critical role in campus leadership. In 2009, Swing wrote that the evolution of the institutional researcher role increasingly shifts to that of change agent—leveraging the capacity to translate data into information and to do so through more direct involvement in institutional decision-making (Swing, 2009). To this end, we present several recommendations institutional researchers can use to develop a more inclusive understanding of military-connected undergraduates and target next steps in institutional policy and practice to support their postsecondary success.

Institutional researchers should disentangle the classification of military-connected students beyond the broad classification of "veteran" and "nonveteran," thereby enabling decision-support efforts to understand how service background may influence the experiences and outcomes of these students. Chapter 3 offers a full-scale codebook in support of this disentanglement, and institutional researchers at institutions taking the first steps toward such efforts can also begin by asking the following question on institutional forms that capture demographic information or on assessment instruments.

*How would you describe your relation to the United States Armed Forces?*

- Dependent (child or spouse) of service member or veteran
- ROTC cadet or NROTC midshipman
- National Guard member
- Reservist
- Active-duty member
- Veteran (no longer on active duty, a reservist, or National Guard member)

Of equal importance to an inclusive identification measure is for institutional researchers to make strategic and meaningful use of these data by engaging stakeholders across campus to target a course of action about how these data can help inform next steps in policy and practice. For instance, IR professionals can stress the importance of disaggregating students who have an affiliation with the military by pointing to differences across military status or other demographic characteristics as they relate to the college experiences and outcomes of these students. Naming a few of many possible indicators, disaggregated data on the financial affordability, student debt, persistence, and attainment rate of military-connected students can provide useful information in the institution's Fact Book or other standard IR reports as well.

Given the differences highlighted in this chapter, it is important that IR professionals study differences to avoid conflating substantive differences that could help campus decision makers to target next steps in the delivery of educational programs and support services to military-connected students. Moreover, institutional researchers should use data to engage with campus stakeholders and inform meaningful discussion about campus strategies to support these students. Appropriate stakeholders may include (a) student affairs professionals; (b) faculty; (c) officials who certify VA/DoD benefits; (d) student veteran support professionals; (e) admissions, enrollment, financial aid, and registrar staff; (f) teaching and learning center staff; (g) administrators; (h) military-connected undergraduates; and (i) community and military/veteran outreach staff. Collectively, these individuals can offer important and varied perspectives on existing support strategies for military-connected undergraduates because they can inform gaps in campuses' understanding of and approach to supporting service members and veterans on campus. On the technical side, they may be able to share information about their campus roles and functions that enable institutional researchers to report information in ways that appropriately accommodate institutional cultures, office structures, and existing campus-wide efforts to support students. To this end, IR professionals can produce information for standing committees with advisory or decision capacities, such as retention and completion task forces or faculty senate-led academic policy committees, that affect the educational opportunities or student support services that impact, but may not be capturing the distinct differences that influence the experiences of military-connected students on campus.

With inclusive identification measures as well as a campus-wide team of individuals invested in the postsecondary success of military-connected undergraduates, it is time for an action plan. These stakeholders can help create an action plan for evidence-based practice to support the post-secondary success of military-connected students across the institution. Evidence that can inform practice can include analyzing the number of military-connected students who persist and complete a college educa-tion within the typical 6-year threshold, and, given the service-related fac-tors known to delay their time-to-degree, it may also be helpful and in-formative to extend the time frame to 8 years or beyond. Such indicators can establish a benchmark for longitudinal comparisons in the persistence and completion rates of military-connected students on campus over time (Student Veterans of America, 2014). Moreover, IR professionals may sur-vey their military-connected students and ask what services and programs have helped them achieve their postsecondary goals. Moreover, institutional researchers should consider accounting for students' military status to un-derstand whether there are differences in the use of programs/services. A set of measures can be defined to assess unmet financial or student ser-vices, efficacy in the delivery of such services, and the extent to which military-connected students attained intended outcomes relative to their civilian peers. These steps serve as helpful tools for the campus to target effective practices while pointing to improvements where they may exist. Finally, stakeholders in the support and success of military-connected stu-dents can share this work among colleagues across campus to strengthen and affirm inclusive practices and support structures for these students. These strategies can ensure that data are used in ways that are student-centered, success-focused, and improvement-oriented.

## Conclusion

In this chapter, we have presented findings that reveal important differences between military-connected students across a number of factors related to college enrollment, persistence, and completion. First, we have shown that military-connected individuals are diverse along demographic and so-cioeconomic lines. Second, we have found that, although the majority of military-connected students apply for and receive aid, the type of aid re-ceived varied by receipt and amount. What was more striking to find was that not all military-connected groups receive VA/DoD education benefits, likely a result of military length-of-service requirements necessary before one becomes eligible to receive VA or DoD benefits. Finally, one of the most substantive findings stemming from the analyses was the high percentage of military-connected undergraduates who face circumstances associated with college noncompletion, particularly among active-duty members.

Taken collectively, these findings underscore important differences across the different categories of military-connected undergraduates on key factors associated with access, success, and noncompletion. In practice, these findings point to important next steps higher education professionals can take to support their postsecondary access and success by painting a more nuanced picture of what differences exist among military-connected undergraduates on campus. Institutional research is critical to gather and present a data-informed narrative enabling the campus community to develop support strategies that appropriately encompass the diverse needs and characteristics of this growing, yet misunderstood, student population.

## References

DiRamio, D., Ackerman, R., & Mitchell, R. L. (2008). From combat to campus: Voices of student veterans. *NASPA Journal, 45*(1), 73–102.

Eighmey, J. (2006). Why do youth enlist? Identification of underlying themes. *Armed Forces & Society, 32*(2), 307–328.

Educational Testing Service. (2000). *The American community college turns 100: A look at its students, programs, and prospects.* Policy Information Center. Princeton, NJ: Coley. Retrieved from https://www.ets.org/Media/Research/pdf/PICCC.pdf

Field, A. (2009). *Discovering statistics using SPSS* (3rd ed.). Thousand Oaks, CA: Sage.

McBain, L., Kim, Y. M., Cook, B., & Snead, K. (2012). *From soldier to student II: Assessing campus programs for veterans and service members.* Washington, DC: ACE, AASCU, NASPA, and NAVPA.

Pallant, J. (2010). *SPSS survival manual* (4th ed.). New York, NY: Open University Press.

Schmid, C., & Abell, P. (2003). Demographic risk factors, study patterns, and campus involvement as related to student success among Guildford Technical Community College students. *Community College Review, 31*(1), 1–16.

Student Veterans of America. (2014). *Million records project: Research from Student Veterans of America.* Washington, DC: Cate. Retrieved from http://studentveterans. org/index.php/what-we-do/million-records-project

Swing, R. (2009). Institutional researchers as change agents. *New Directions for Institutional Research, 143,* 5–16.

U.S. Department of Education. (1995). *Profile of undergraduates in U.S. postsecondary education institutions: 1992–1993.* National Center for Education Statistics. Washington, DC: Horn & Premo. Retrieved from http://nces.ed.gov/pubs/96237.pdf

U.S. Department of Education. (2002). *Nontraditional Undergraduates.* National Center for Education Statistics. Washington, DC: Choy. Retrieved from https://nces.ed. gov/pubs2002/2002012.pdf

U.S. Department of Education. (2009). *Beginning Postsecondary Student Longitudinal Study.* Datalab for Postsecondary Education. Author analyses of QuickStats data tables.

U.S. Department of Education. (2011). *Six-Year Attainment, Persistence, Transfer, Retention, and Withdrawal Rates of Students Who Began Postsecondary Education in 2003–04.* National Center for Education Statistics. Washington, DC: Skomsvold, Radford, & Berkner. Retrieved from http://nces.ed.gov/pubs2011/2011152.pdf

U.S. Department of Education. (2015). *NPSAS Undergraduate Codebook*. National Center for Education Statistics. Washington, DC. Retrieved from http://nces.ed.gov/datalab/powerstats/pdf/npsas2012ug_subject.pdf

U.S. Department of Veterans Affairs. (2015, July 29). *Education service update*. Presentation conducted at the Western Association of Veterans Education Specialists (WAVES) 2015 Conference, Anaheim, CA. Retrieved from http://uswaves.org/images/2015/final/Education_Service_Update.pdf

Woodruff, T., Kelty, R., & Segal, D. R. (2006). Propensity to serve and motivation to enlist among American combat soldiers. *Armed Forces and Society 32*(3), 353–366.

Zinger, L., & Cohen, A. (2010). Veterans returning from war into the classroom: How can colleges be better prepared to meet their needs. *Contemporary Issues in Education Research, 3*(1), 39–51.

DANI MOLINA *is director of the Veterans Resource Center at California State University, Los Angeles.*

ANDREW Q. MORSE *is consultant and project director, Keeling & Associates, LLC.*

5

*This chapter explores the lack of data about student veterans and reasons this lack of data raises particular concerns about for-profit institutions, which enroll a large percentage of student veterans.*

# For-Profit Institutions and Student Veteran Data

*Kevin C. Jones, Bonnie K. Fox Garrity*

Since its inception in 1944, the G.I. Bill has subsidized higher education tuition for thousands of military veterans. Although state universities, community colleges, and private nonprofit schools have been the overwhelming participants in this revolutionary program, since the beginning of the wars in Iraq and Afghanistan, and particularly after the passage of the Post-9/11 G.I. Bill in 2009, for-profit (or proprietary) colleges have made exceptional advancement into the student veteran higher education space. Despite the fact that only 31% of student veterans attend proprietary colleges, a significant percentage of G.I. Bill funding flows to these schools and their cost, on average, is much higher than public universities and state community colleges (National Center for Education Statistics [NCES], 2015). In 2010, revenue from military education at the 20 largest for-profit colleges reached $521.2 million (Zillman, 2014).

By 2013, 31% of all student veterans attended a for-profit school, with proprietary institutions holding 8 of the top 10 spots for post-9/11 G.I. Bill recipients nationwide (Zillman, 2014). To put this number in perspective, in 2012 the for-profit educational sector as a whole accounted for 13.3% of all postsecondary enrollments (Deming, Goldin, & Katz, 2012). In the 2012–2013 academic year, for-profit colleges and universities brought in over $1.7 billion from G.I. Bill funds alone, a remarkable increase despite ongoing regulatory political pressure from Congress and the White House (S. Rep. No. 112–137, 2012). Since 2010, 40% of G.I. Bill benefits have gone to the for-profit education sector (Wong, 2015). In California, the University of Phoenix's San Diego campus has received more G.I. Bill funding than the University of California's entire 10-campus system and extension programs combined (Glantz, 2014). Of the $1.5 billion in G.I. Bill funding received by California colleges and universities between 2009 and 2014, 40% ($638

New Directions for Institutional Research, no. 171 © 2017 Wiley Periodicals, Inc.
Published online in Wiley Online Library (wileyonlinelibrary.com) • DOI: 10.1002/ir.20195

million) went to schools that had failed to meet state financial aid standards during the previous 4-year period (Jordan, 2015).

Despite media and political attention regarding for-profit colleges and universities, there remains a great deal of speculation—but little introspective, peer-reviewed, scholarly data—about veteran experiences at these institutions. For these reasons, it is important that researchers, policy makers, and students themselves have access to accurate, specific, and verifiable information about this sector of higher education.

This chapter explores the reasons student veterans may enroll at for-profit institutions in higher percentages than not-for-profit or public institutions, including characteristics of student veterans, unique characteristics of for-profit institutions, and restrictions that may encourage for-profit institutions to enroll student veterans. We then discuss expense structures of for-profit institutions and costs of the veteran aid programs in the context of a lack of outcome data. This chapter will help the reader to articulate the reasons for concern about these enrollment patterns and consider the role of institutional researchers in addressing the issue of a lack of data about student veterans on all campuses.

## Student Veterans

Student veterans are more likely than their civilian peers to be first-generation college students (Lang & Powers, 2011) with 66% of prior-enlisted service members being the first in their family to attend higher education of any kind compared to 32% of students overall (National Survey of Student Engagement, 2010; National Center for Education Statistics, 2012). With their "more sharply defined career goals" and prior military responsibilities and life experiences, veterans often find undergraduate student culture "unproductive" at residential colleges and universities (DiRamio & Jarvis, 2011). Because of these and other conditions, both academic as well as co-curricular, student veterans are more likely to seek out technical and career-oriented programs—exactly the kind of programs offered by for-profit institutions. For student veterans, the G.I. Bill is more than a way to pay for tuition. It has "served as a hyperbaric chamber to adjust to civilian life, allowing [student veterans] to stay busy and avoid poverty as they set out to find a post-military career" (Chandrasekaran, 2014, para. 59).

## For-Profit, Not-for-Profit, and Public Institutions

All institutions must be authorized by the state to provide postsecondary education to obtain Title IV aid eligibility under the Higher Education Act. However, as corporations, institutions are required to comply with different federal and state rules depending on whether they are not-for-profit, public, or for-profit. Not-for-profit and public institutions register with the state and are required to serve the public good. They receive revenue from

NEW DIRECTIONS FOR INSTITUTIONAL RESEARCH • DOI: 10.1002/ir

multiple sources including tuition, donations, and direct government appropriations; their nondistribution constraint dictates that they are not allowed to distribute excess revenue to those who control the institution. For-profit institutions are unique in that they are not required to serve the public good, they receive a majority, if not all, of their revenue from tuition and fees (Knapp, Kelly-Reid, & Ginder, 2012), and they are not subject to the nondistribution constraint, so excess revenue generated may be distributed to those who own or control the institution (Winston, 1999b). These different constraints provide an increased incentive for for-profit providers to enroll students whose tuition is publicly funded by the Department of Veterans Affairs (VA) programs or military tuition assistance to increase revenue. Many institutions prefer public funding as it is guaranteed revenue.

## Funding Constraints

For-profit providers have additional constraints beyond those imposed on public or not-for-profit institutions participating in VA and military programs. For example, to participate in Post-9/11 G.I. Bill funding for veterans, regular, accredited degree programs at public and not-for-profit colleges are "deemed approved," which means that there is no review or approval required from a state approving agency for these programs to receive G.I. Bill funds, although new schools seeking approval are required to file an application. In contrast, all programs at for-profit colleges must be approved through a VA-designated state approval agency. This approval requires a review with a focus on the financial soundness of the institution and institutional enrollment limitations.

Additional limitations on the amount of revenue that can be generated from publicly funded sources also exist. All institutions are subject to the 85–15 rule for participation in Post-9/11 G.I. Bill funding. This rule states that veteran enrollment cannot exceed 85% of the students in a program (Veteran's Benefits—Disapproval of Enrollment in Certain Courses, 2006). This is based on the assumption that high-quality programs should be able to produce 15% of their income from nongovernment sources (Mitchell, 2015).

Other public funding sources place limits exclusively on for-profit institutions. The 90–10 rule in the Higher Education Act states that for-profit institutions may receive no more than 90% of their revenue from Title IV aid programs such as Pell grants and subsidized student loans (The Higher Education Act of 1965 as amended, 1965). However, veterans' benefits and military tuition assistance currently do not count toward the 90%; therefore, recruitment of veterans is an important source of public funding to ensure compliance with the 90–10 rule. For example, in order to gain "market penetration" into the lucrative student veteran demographic, the University of Phoenix allocated significant funding to portray itself as a friend to the armed forces, including sponsoring concerts and morale, welfare, and

NEW DIRECTIONS FOR INSTITUTIONAL RESEARCH • DOI: 10.1002/ir

recreation (MWR) events at military bases (Glanz, 2015). When combined with traditional advertising this strategy helped enable the university to capture $345 million in G.I. Bill funding in 2014 and $1.2 billion since 2009 (Glanz, 2015).

Neither veterans' benefit nor Title IV programs will allow themselves, individually, to be the sole funding source of a for-profit institution; however, if both programs are utilized in combination, a for-profit institution could conceivably become 100% publicly funded. Unlike their public and nonprofit counterparts, a 100% publicly funded for-profit institution is not required to serve the public good and may legally distribute excess revenue to those who own and control the institution. Title IV funding, including Pell grants, is handled administratively by the Department of Education, and the G.I. Bill is managed by the Department of Veterans Affairs. Absent mandate or existing ability to share data regarding student veteran finances readily, it is impossible to tell whether or not any institutions are being solely funded with public, taxpayer dollars in this manner.

An additional incentive to recruit veterans is created by the interplay between veterans' benefits and the cohort default rate (CDR) rule. Under this rule, an institution will lose eligibility to participate in Higher Education Act Title IV aid programs (e.g., Pell grants, federal student loans) if more than 30% of students who graduated from an institution default on their student loans in three consecutive years. This is meant to encourage high-quality programs whose graduates earn enough income to pay their student loans. Because veterans have access to grant aid, they are less likely to take out large student loans. Therefore, they are less likely to default on student loans, thus assisting a program in remaining in compliance with the cohort default rate rule without the necessity of an institution investing in improved quality of programs (Nelson, 2014). This encourages institutions that are at risk of failing the cohort default rate measure to enroll additional student veterans. Because the average Federal student loan debt of a student at a 4-year-and-above for-profit institution ($24,314) is twice that of a student at a 4-year-and-above not-for-profit ($12,495) and nearly three times higher than a student at a 4-year-and-above public ($9,572) (U.S. Department of Education, 2014), for-profit institutions have the greatest incentive to recruit veterans to offset this cohort default rate risk.

## Why Veterans' Benefits Cost More at Not-for-Profit and For-Profit Institutions

Enrollment of a student veteran at a not-for-profit or for-profit institution may be more costly to taxpayers than if that same student enrolled at a public institution. For example, under the Post-9/11 G.I. Bill (also known as chapter 33 benefits), the maximum payment for tuition and fees for a student enrolled at a public institution is the total tuition and fees for an in-state student. At a not-for-profit or for-profit institution, the maximum rate is $21,084.89 for tuition and fees during the 2015–2016 academic year (VA, 2015a). Although individual programs or campuses of public institutions may charge in-state tuition and fees higher than the annual maximum rate, the highest average in-state tuition at a public institution is approximately $11,500, a figure that is about half of the maximum rate for not-for-profit and for-profit institutions (VA, 2015a).

In addition, institutions may enter into a voluntary agreement with the Department of Veterans Affairs to participate in the Yellow Ribbon Program, which provides additional funding for eligible students at for-profit and not-for-profit schools if their tuition is above the cost of public, in-state tuition covered by the Post-9/11 G.I. Bill. Under this program, the institution agrees to contribute 50% of the tuition and fees that exceed the maximum cap and the VA matches the amount provided by the institution. Payments of over $179 million were made to institutions under the Yellow Ribbon program during fiscal year 2014. Over $54 million, or 30% of Yellow Ribbon aid, was paid to for-profit institutions.

Student veterans may be eligible to receive a monthly housing stipend and a book stipend in addition to tuition and fees. These costs are not differentiated, so the taxpayer cost of these benefits is the same regardless of institutional type.

## Expense Structures

For-profit institutions operate differently than not-for-profit or public institutions. They tend to offer career-focused programs that require fewer capital resources. They spend less on instruction than not-for-profit and public institutions by using expense-minimization strategies to maintain lower expenses. These strategies may include employing a large number of adjunct faculty, implementing standardized courses and curricula, operating in leased spaces to avoid the fixed costs of building ownership and maintenance, offering fewer athletic programs, and employing limited full-time faculty whose time is devoted solely to teaching, with no research or shared governance activities (Bennett, Lucchesi, & Vedder, 2010; Kelly, 2001; Kinser, 2006a, 2006b; Morey, 2004; Turner, 2006). These strategies result in a flexible expense structure that maintains a stable, low expense per full-time equivalent student. By contrast, not-for-profit and public institutions tend to have a relatively level amount of total expenses that do not vary significantly based on enrollment. This allows for-profit institutions to adjust more rapidly to a changing environment.

In addition, for-profit institutions will offer programs of study where the tuition levels will more than cover the expense of providing the program. This is important because for-profit institutions receive a majority of their revenue from tuition and fees. Winston (1999a) and Kelly (2001) suggested that for-profits engage in "functional cherry picking" where they offer programs with the greatest difference between expenses and revenue.

By contrast, not-for-profit and public institutions tend to subsidize each student's education by providing programs that have higher expenses than tuition revenue (Winston, 1999b). Donated resources and governmental funding (e.g., state appropriations, federal research grants, etc.) provide for the difference. Therefore, the expense incurred by an institution for a student's education is higher than the cost that the student pays at a not-for-profit or public institution. At a for-profit institution, the opposite is often true. A student's tuition is higher than the amount spent on the student's education and the student subsidizes the institution. In addition, because of the lack of a nondistribution constraint, excess tuition revenue generated at a for-profit institution may be distributed to owners, managers, and shareholders as profit. Therefore, at a for-profit institution, a portion of publicly funded tuition aid such as veterans' educational benefits may not be spent on the student's education and instead may be distributed to those who control the institution. In fact, some institutions have been found to spend less money on instructional expenses for all students combined than the amount of publicly funded Pell grants received (Fox Garrity, Garrison, & Fiedler, 2010).

Although instructional expenses are minimized, some for-profits spend a large portion of their budgets on selling and promotional activities, such as the Apollo Group, which spent 33% of its budget on these activities in 2009 (Bennett et al., 2010). These expenses are funded with tuition dollars. Unsurprisingly, spending more money on marketing and less money on instruction has not translated into higher official graduation rates at for-profit institutions. The official measure is limited to first-time, full-time freshmen, which is a small fraction of the students at most for-profit institutions; however, these are the only reported graduation rates available for comparison. Among students who began their bachelor's degree program in Fall 2006, the graduation rate was 32% at for-profits, 66% at not-for-profits, and 57% at publics (U.S. Department of Education National Center for Education Statistics, 2014).

Students at 4-year-and-above for-profit institutions have the highest loan default rate. The 3-year cohort default rates for 2011 were 18.6% at for-profits, 7.0% at not-for-profits, and 8.9% at publics (U.S. Department of Education National Center for Education Statistics, 2015). Loan default rates are often considered a proxy measure of program quality, as it is assumed that students who graduate with a high-value degree will earn an income sufficient to facilitate loan repayment.

Financial variations by institutional type drive operational differences among for-profit, not-for-profit, and public institutions. These operational differences result in varied student outcomes including lower average bachelor's degree graduation rates and higher average loan default rates for students who attend for-profit institutions (Deming, Golden, & Katz, 2013). Although individual institutional results may vary widely from the averages, inferior average outcomes at for-profits are achieved, and a portion of the veteran and military aid meant to assist students in funding their educations may be spent on marketing activities and distributed to those who control the institution in the form of profit. Although all institutions should track and report student veteran data, it is particularly important that for-profit institutions diligently track and report information on costs and student outcomes given the additional risks presented by for-profit structures.

## Student Veteran Data

Outcomes in the form of graduation rates and loan default rates are proxy measures of student learning and program quality that do not capture the entirety of a student's educational experience. The lack of specific data regarding educational outcomes for student veterans creates a situation where enrolling veterans can result in income from public money for an institution with little or no external accountability for actual results. Because potential students have less information about the education they will receive prior to enrolling than the providing institution, there is an information asymmetry between the student and the institution.

This asymmetry of information between an institution and the student is an issue at all types of institutions, including for-profits; lack of concrete data regarding student veteran persistence and success across all sectors of higher education is an ongoing concern. The G.I. Bill, unlike Title IV federal education funding, is distributed via the Department of Veterans Affairs (VA) rather than the Department of Education (ED). Because of the VA's focus on G.I. Bill disbursement rather than veteran academic performance and outcomes, there are little federal data regarding how veterans perform in higher education. In an effort to address this issue, Student Veterans of America (SVA), a national nonprofit advocacy group, conducted the "Million Records Project," designed to compile accurate, comprehensive data regarding veteran performance in higher education on a national scale (SVA, 2014). Despite the strong efforts to compile student veteran data across the higher education spectrum, information regarding for-profit institutions was found to be unreliable because of that sector's chronic underrepresentation in the National Student Clearinghouse, a voluntary reporting system used to provide much of the Million Records' data (McCann, 2014).

Trust in the provider is an important element when data are lacking. Both Winston (1999b) and Hansmann (1981) argue that not-for-profit organizations are preferable in these circumstances for three reasons. One is that the nondistribution constraint requires that excess revenue be reinvested in the goods or services being produced rather than possibly being distributed to shareholders/owners as profits or dividends, allowing for a comfort level for the party to the transaction that their money will eventually be used for the intended purpose. A second reason is the potential for fraud where such an information asymmetry exists. The inability of a not-for-profit to generate profits for owners reduces one source of pressure to engage in

NEW DIRECTIONS FOR INSTITUTIONAL RESEARCH • DOI: 10.1002/ir

fraudulent activities that take advantage of the asymmetry of information in the transaction. Third, Hansmann (2012) suggested that not-for-profits have the incentive of personal pride and satisfaction of managers, which encourages them to offer higher-quality products and services, particularly when demand increases. For these reasons, the lack of specific data regarding outcomes for student veterans at all types of institutions is more troubling in the context of for-profit institutions.

## G.I. Bill Feedback System

In January 2014, the VA, in partnership with the Department of Defense and Department of Education, created the G.I. Bill Feedback System in order to create a consumer protection measure for those receiving education benefits (including the G.I. Bill) (VA, 2015a). Between January and November of 2014, 1,434 complaints about postsecondary institutions were received. Of those, the VA has closed 312, with the remaining complaints still being investigated (VA, 2015a). With what the administration termed "the most serious complaints," the VA conducted 42 targeted risk-based program reviews: 4 at public institutions, 2 at not-for-profit private institutions, and 36 (85% of targeted program reviews) at for-profit institutions of higher education. The three organizations with the highest number of complaints were the University of Phoenix, DeVry/Keller, and ITT Technical Institute, all for-profit schools, the latter of which went out of business in September, 2016, in large part because of sanctions imposed by the Department of Education (Smith, 2016). Part of this is undoubtedly due to the sheer size of these institutions (University of Phoenix, for example, is the largest university in the United States, with 256,402 students as of 2012, 43,301 of whom are veterans (NCES, 2015).

However, complaint-based control systems are reactive in nature and provide minimal protection for current student veterans. The premise of these systems is that in order for an institution to face negative consequences, a student or students must be harmed, the student must become aware of that harm, and then the student files a complaint (VA, 2015b). In the meantime, multiple other student veterans may have been subject to this same harm. For example, if the complaint is about transferability of credits, due to the information asymmetry between the student and the institution, the student will not become aware that his or her credits may not transfer to an institution of choice until after completing the courses or degree program. The elapsed time from enrollment to the realization of harm could be years. The reactive, complaint-based system is a slow process that will allow many other student veterans to be harmed before a complaint is filed or resolved. Unfortunately, because veterans' educational benefits are not replenished after a case of institutional fraud, all of the student veterans who attended the institution in the meantime, and the public who funded those benefits, lose out on the money that was paid to that institution.

## The Role of Institutional Researchers

Institutional researchers, as student data caretakers often directly involved with organizational strategic planning and policy, have an opportunity to rectify the lack of available data regarding student veterans. The Florida College System, for example, recently added a requirement that all students must be asked to specify their military/veteran status when registering at any of the state's 28 state and community colleges. This information is then entered into Florida's Student Database, giving researchers a population they can break down by military, veteran, and dependent status. Although voluntary, and only in its first year of use, adding this variable to state higher education records is a simple addition that will allow researchers to compile longitudinal data regarding how student veterans perform in Florida higher education. As detailed in Chapter 6, Virginia, through the State Council of Higher Education for Virginia (SCHEV), has a robust postsecondary longitudinal data system that serves as an example of what state-level data systems should aspire to. Information tracked includes veteran status for every student at every higher education institution in the state, with the notable exception of for-profit schools. Lack of publically available data from proprietary institutions will continue to be a roadblock for research and accountability unless state and federal agencies intervene to change current regulations and require transparency.

## Conclusion

Institutions operate in an environment with limited reporting of data and few proactive controls in place to access public funding through the enrollment of student veterans. For-profit institutions operate with a different set of constraints and priorities than not-for-profit and public institutions. Because for-profit institutions can distribute funds to those who own and control the institution and are not required to serve the public good, public funds provided for the education of student veterans can be transferred to those who control the institution as private wealth. When considered within an environment characterized by a lack of reliable, comparable data related to student veteran experiences at institutions, the increasing enrollment of student veterans at for-profit institutions raises special concerns. Understanding the differences among institutional types is absolutely critical as controls and data systems are designed to ensure that student veterans receive the greatest possible value from their educational benefits.

## References

Bennett, D., Lucchesi, A., & Vedder, R. (2010). *For-profit higher education: Growth, innovation and regulation.* Washington, DC: Center for College Affordability and Productivity.

Chandrasekaran, R. (2014, March 29). A legacy of pain and pride. *The Washington Post*. Retrieved from http://www.washingtonpost.com/sf/national/2014/03/29/a-legacy-of-pride-and-pain/

Deming, D., Goldin, C., & Katz, L. (2013). For-profit colleges. *The Future of Children*, 23(1), 137–163.

Deming, D. J., Goldin, C., & Katz, L. F. (2012). The for-profit postsecondary school sector: Nimble critters or agile predators? *Journal of Economic Perspectives*, 26(1), 139–164.

DiRamio, D., & Jarvis, K. (2011). When Johnny and Jane come marching to campus. *ASHE Higher Education Report*, 37(3).

Fox Garrity, B., Garrison, M., & Fiedler, R. (2010). Access for whom, access to what? The role of the "disadvantaged student" market in the rise of for-profit higher education in the U.S. *Journal of Critical Education Policy Studies*, 8(1), 203–244.

Glantz, A. (2014, June 28). *GI Bill funds flow to for-profit colleges that fail state aid standards*. Retrieved from Center for Investigative Reporting website: http://cironline.org/reports/gi-bill-funds-flow-profit-colleges-fail-state-aid-standards-6477

Glanz, A. (2015, June 30). *University of Phoenix sidesteps Obama order on recruiting veterans*. Retrieved from Center for Investigative Reporting website: https://www.revealnews.org/article/university-of-phoenix-sidesteps-obama-order-on-recruiting-veterans/

Hansmann, H. (1981). The rationale for exempting nonprofit organizations from corporate income tax. *The Yale Law Journal*, 91(1), 54–100.

Hansmann, H. (2012). The evolving economic structure of higher education. *The University of Chicago Law Review*, 79, 159–183.

The Higher Education Act of 1965 as amended, U.S.C. 20 (1965).

Jordan, B. (2015, February 11). *Budget proposal restricts GI Bill funding to for-profit colleges*. Retrieved from http://www.military.com/daily-news/2015/02/11/budget-proposal-restricts-gi-bill-funding-to-for-profit-colleges.html

Kelly, K. (2001). Meeting needs and making profits: The rise of for-profit degree-granting institutions. *ECS Issue Paper*. Denver, CO: Educational Commission of the States.

Kinser, K. (2006a). From Main Street to Wall Street. *ASHE Higher Education Report*, 31(5), 1–146.

Kinser, K. (2006b). What Phoenix doesn't teach us about for-profit higher education. *Change*, 38(4), 24–29.

Knapp, L., Kelly-Reid, J., & Ginder, S. (2012). *Enrollment in postsecondary institutions, fall 2011; financial statistics, fiscal year 2011; and graduation rates, selected cohorts, 2003–2008*. Washington, DC: U.S. Department of Education.

Lang, W. A., & Powers, J. T. (2011). *Competing the mission: A pilot study of veterans' student progress toward degree attainment in the post-9/11 era* [White paper]. Retrieved from http://www.operationpromiseforservicemembers.com/Completing_the_Mission_Nov20

McCann, C. (2014, April 8). *Million Records Project raises as many questions as answers*. Retrieved from http://www.edcentral.org/million-records-project-raises-many-questions-answers/1.pdf

Mitchell, T. (2015). *Open Letter to service members and veterans from U.S. Under Secretary of Education Ted Mitchell to our service members and veterans*. Retrieved from http://www.ed.gov/news/press-releases/open-letter-service-members-and-veterans-us-under-secretary-education-ted-mitchell-our-service-members-and-veterans.

Morey, A. (2004). Globalization and the emergence of for-profit higher education. *Higher Education*, 48(1), 131–150.

National Center for Education Statistics. (2015). *National postsecondary student aid study (NPSAS)*. Washington, DC: Author.

National Survey of Student Engagement. (2010). *Major differences: Examining student engagement by field of study*. Bloomington, IN: Indiana University Center for Postsecondary Research.

Nelson, M. A. (2014). Never ascribe to malice that which is adequately explained by incompetence: A failure to protect student veterans. *Journal of College and University Law, 40*(159), 1–29.

S. Rep. 112 – 137, vol 1 – 4 (2012)

Smith, A. A. (2016, September 7). *The end for ITT Tech*. Retrieved from https://www.insidehighered.com/news/2016/09/07/itt-tech-shuts-down-all-campuses

Student Veterans of America. (2014). *Million Records Project*. Retrieved from http://studentveterans.org/index.php/what-we-do/million-records-project

Turner, S. (2006). For-profit colleges in the context of the market for higher education. In D. Breneman, B. Pusser, & S. Turner (Eds.), *Earnings from learning: The rise of for-profit universities* (pp. 51–68). Albany, NY: State University of New York.

U.S. Department of Education. (2014). *Fiscal year 2014 budget proposal student loans overview*. Washington, DC: Author.

U.S. Department of Education National Center for Education Statistics. (2014). Institutional retention and graduation rates for undergraduate students. *The Condition of Education 2014*.

U.S. Department of Education National Center for Education Statistics. (2015). Student loan volume and default rates. *The Condition of Education*.

U.S. Department of Veterans Affairs. (2015a). *GI bill feedback system*. Retrieved from http://www.benefits.va.gov/GIBILL/Feedback.asp

U.S. Department of Veterans Affairs. (2015b). *Post-9/11 GI Bill (Chapter 33) payment rates for 2015 academic year (August 1, 2015–July 31, 2016)*. Retrieved from http://www.benefits.va.gov/GIBILL/resources/benefits_resources/rates/ch33/ch33rates080115.asp

Veteran's Benefits—Disapproval of Enrollment in Certain Courses, 38 U.S.C. § 3680A(d)(1) (2006).

Winston, G. (1999a). For-profit higher education: Godzilla or Chicken Little? *Change, 31*(1), 12–20.

Winston, G. (1999b). Subsidies, hierarchy, and peers: The awkward economics of higher education. *Journal of Economic Perspectives, 13*(1), 13–36.

Wong, A. (2015, June 24). 'Dollar signs in uniform': Why for-profit colleges target veterans. *The Atlantic*. Retrieved from http://www.theatlantic.com/education/archive/2015/06/for-profit-college-veterans-loophole/396731/

Zillman, C. (2014, November 11). For profit colleges still reap millions from veterans GI Bill. *Fortune*. Retrieved from http://fortune.com/2014/11/11/gi-bill-for-profit-colleges/

KEVIN C. JONES *is a former United States Marine and current director of strategic planning and assessment at Polk State College in Florida.*

BONNIE K. FOX GARRITY *is a professor of business and the director of internal affairs of the Veteran and Military Affiliated Research Center (VMARC) at D'Youville College in Buffalo, NY.*

*6*

*This chapter describes the benefits and challenges of state-level longitudinal data collection on student veterans and offers recommendations for optimizing collection and reporting for the advocacy of student veteran success.*

# Exploring Veteran Success Through State-Level Administrative Data Sets

*Tod Massa, Laura Gogia*

Since the enactment of the Post-9/11 Veterans Assistance Act of 2008 (commonly known as the Post-9/11 G.I. Bill) more than 1 million beneficiaries have accessed funding, including full (for in-state, public institutions) or supplemental (for out-of-state and private institutions) coverage of tuition and fees, housing, and book expenses (McBain, Kim, Cook, & Snead, 2012). In 2013 alone, the federal government invested $10.8 billion in Post-9/11 G.I. Bill benefits for almost 800,000 veterans (Student Veterans of America, 2014). Despite this massive investment of funding, little has been reported about related financial need, academic performance, or workforce-related outcomes. Although a majority of public colleges and universities (74% and 66% of public 4- and 2-year institutions, respectively) have programming specifically for student veterans, few provide outcome data related to their student veteran persistence or success (O'Herrin, 2011). Furthermore, the federal government currently collects only information on student veteran enrollment and related funding disbursement. The Million Records Report, published by the Student Veterans of America in 2014, is a significant exception; researchers supported through a private–public collaboration matched 1 million records from the U.S. Department of Veterans Affairs and the National Student Clearinghouse to calculate a 51.7% graduation rate and an average time-to-completion of 5.1 years for an associate degree and 6.3 years for a bachelor's degree among student veterans who accessed Montgomery G.I. Bill or Post-9/11 G.I. Bill funding between 2002 and 2010 (Cate, 2014).

Promoting student veteran success in higher education requires the collection and analysis of more comprehensive data than is currently accessible. Longitudinal data systems (LDS) and statewide longitudinal data systems (SLDS) can augment institutional and federal data collection to provide a more systematic and nuanced approach to understanding the

New Directions for Institutional Research, no. 171 © 2017 Wiley Periodicals, Inc.
Published online in Wiley Online Library (wileyonlinelibrary.com) • DOI: 10.1002/ir.20196

87

educational pathways associated with student veteran success. Data collection needs to begin with total enrollment counts—which are often missing at institutional and state levels—but then extend to data elements that speak to financial need, student experience, degree completion, and post-completion employment. This chapter, with Virginia used as an example, will discuss the potential for and barriers to good state-level data collection before suggesting strategies for collecting and reporting meaningful data on student veteran success.

## Statewide Longitudinal Data Collection: LDS and SLDS

Statewide longitudinal data collection can be performed at three levels of scope. The first is a longitudinal data system (LDS), defined as a system that collects individual-level data from institutional administrative systems and reports it out in aggregated form at a statewide level (Ewell, 1995). Typically, LDS are restricted to a single sector. For example, the State Council of Higher Education for Virginia (SCHEV) supports a postsecondary longitudinal data system based on the student data model developed by the National Center for Higher Education Management Systems (Ewell, 1995). Although the LDS is limited to the postsecondary context, it provides easy access to information on financial need, enrollment, progress, and outcomes for students enrolled in all Virginia 2- and 4-year public and nonprofit private institutions. The system has the capacity to support a diverse number of queries based on time period, institutional profile, and student demographics, cohort, or sub-cohort.

Recently, advances in technology and trends in government policy have allowed for the development of state-level longitudinal data systems (SLDS), "unit-level data systems designed for collection, management, analysis, and reporting of statewide education data over time and across programs" (U.S. Department of Education, 2015, p. 31). SLDS is generally reserved to describe a collection of LDS that spans educational sectors, usually some combination of early learning, K–12, postsecondary, and workforce entities. The purpose of SLDS is to assist in the identification and promotion of successful pathways within the education-to-workforce pipeline. SLDS may be centralized or federated; the former creates a data mart or some other single system to collect and store all the individual unit data from SLDS agency partners, and the latter leaves the data within the home-agency LDS, accessing only what it needs for a specific query to the SLDS (Education Commission of the States, 2016).

Finally, some SLDS extend in scope beyond the education-to-workforce pipeline because of the nature of their partnering agencies. The Virginia Longitudinal Data System (VLDS; http://vlds.virginia.gov) offers an example of a federated SLDS that connects data from educational and noneducational sectors. As of 2016, VLDS partners included the Virginia Department of Education (VDOE), the State Council of Higher Education for Virginia

(SCHEV), the Virginia Employment Commission (VEC), the Virginia Department of Social Services (VDSS), the workforce division of the Virginia Community College System (VCCS), the Virginia Department for Aging and Rehabilitative Services (DARS), and Virginia Department of Health Professions (DHP). The system is designed to expand for the inclusion of additional partners.

## The Value of Statewide Data Collection

Statewide longitudinal data collection via LDS or SLDS adds significant value to individual institutional data because it links data already collected by institutions to expand our understanding of student veteran needs and success, to promote higher education, and to advance broader statewide goals. Unlike institutional-level data systems, statewide longitudinal data collection is not limited by a single institutional context, so it facilitates the study of student (or citizen) actions whether they engage with single or multiple institutions. The ability to track person flow through and across institutions allows for a better understanding of the big picture: relationships between institutions, interactions between sectors, and patterns of student behavior (by cohort, demographics, and subcohorts). Moreover, because LDS and SLDS are overseen by state policy makers rather than individual institutional administrators, they may be used with broader, more comprehensive, or powerful mandates than those afforded to individual institutional research units.

**For Student Veterans.**    Student veterans are, by definition, nontraditional students. Available statistics suggest student veterans are more likely than the average undergraduate student to be older (greater than 25 years of age), to be persons of color, and to be independents with families of their own (O'Herrin, 2011). Additionally, many student veterans have special needs related to their military experience. Radford (2009) estimated that at least 14–19% of student veterans have formal diagnoses of posttraumatic stress disorder, traumatic brain injury, or depression. Many more are dealing with the complex psycho-socioeconomic transition of returning to civilian life. The ability of LDS and SLDS to capture fits and starts within an academic career or enrollments across multiple institutions is particularly important when studying nontraditional student cohorts such as student veterans, who are more likely to engage the educational system in these behaviors than traditional undergraduate students (Cate, 2014; O'Herrin, 2011).

**For Higher Education.**    As federal- and state level policy makers consider education and workforce as a holistic entity or pipeline, SLDS are becoming increasingly essential to the development and implementation of higher education policy. In the past, following the flow of individual students or sub-cohorts across institutions or sectors would not have been

NEW DIRECTIONS FOR INSTITUTIONAL RESEARCH • DOI: 10.1002/ir

possible. Now SLDS allow more reliable means for capturing timing and choices made in the pipeline.

The value of SLDS has not gone unrecognized by state or federal governments. The U.S. Department of Education has granted over $265 million to 41 states and the District of Columbia to develop SLDS that can connect at least some educational sectors with workforce (U.S. Department of Education, 2009). As of 2016, the Education Commission of the States found that all 50 states and the District of Columbia have the ability to link sectors, with 37 connecting data across at least two of the four primary sectors of interest (early learning, K–12, postsecondary and workforce). Sixteen states and the District of Columbia have already implemented full P20W data systems.

**For Statewide Goals.** When SLDS partnership agreements are opened up to sectors beyond education and workforce, the types of questions answered by the system expand beyond the education to workforce pipeline. The Virginia SLDS (VLDS) offers an example of the value added through inclusiveness. Current questions being studied with VLDS-generated data include the impact of health, social service, education, and workforce pipeline on Virginia's economy; return on investment of health, social service, education, and workforce opportunities and programs; alignment of health, social service, education, and workforce programs to known and projected employers' needs; collective, long-term impact of health, social service, education, and workforce programs on people served; pathways to the workforce; patterns of employment; factors or conditions that predict success; and factors or conditions that have the greatest impact on educational achievement and later productivity (VLDS, n.d.).

## Barriers to Data Collection SLDS: Policy and Resource Allocation

Nevertheless, the presence of well-established LDS and SLDS cannot overcome all of the barriers to comprehensive data collection that are created by policy and resource allocation. As previously described, Virginia serves as a national exemplar for state-level collection for longitudinal systems, with a postsecondary LDS since 1992 and VLDS since 2009. However, the State Council of Higher Education for Virginia, which administers the postsecondary LDS and VLDS, cannot reliably identify student veterans within Virginia institutions of higher education, nor can it provide any information on common measures of success, such as retention, time to completion, or graduation rates. VLDS cannot track student veteran progress through the education-to-workforce pipeline, nor can it provide data on the interactions between veteran use of state-level social services and institutions of higher education.

In Virginia, the lack of data on student veterans does not demonstrate a failure in intellectual or logistical capacity, but rather limitations related to the orientation of public policy and resource allocation. Statewide data collection requires time, skilled personnel, and technology at the institutional and state level. Therefore, agencies tend to add elements to data collection only when there is a clear legislative mandate. Furthermore, state policy makers will allocate funds for data collection only when the resultant information is directly related to the creation, modification, or implementation of state code. Therefore, the content and orientation of state policy will dictate the types of information collected by state agencies.

In the instance of U.S. military personnel and higher education, Virginia law is limited to protecting in-state residency status and tuition benefits for active military, veterans, National Guardspersons, and family members within Virginia colleges and universities, with various stipulations (Commonwealth of Virginia, 2016). Therefore, all student veteran data collected at a statewide level relates to the tracking of the disbursement of these funds.

The narrow focus on fund disbursement impacts the quality of the data collection in two ways. First, the resultant data collection fails to identify all student veterans enrolled in Virginia institutions of higher education. Relying on tuition codes to identify and follow student veterans in Virginia institutions of higher education fails to include students who qualify for Virginia residency under other criteria, including those who never gave up their Virginia residency status during their service or those who have established Virginia residency after service.

Second, none of the data collected speak to performance measures of student veterans, nor do they demonstrate the connections between access, affordability, and performance that are experienced by student veterans and impacted by the programs that aim to serve them. The history of Pell grant reporting in Virginia serves as a relevant example. Pell grants, as well as other Title IV financial aid programs (Office of Federal Student Aid, n.d.) resemble the Post-9/11 G.I. Bill in that they are federal programs designed to increase access to higher education for populations who might otherwise have issues of accessibility or affordability. In Virginia, SCHEV began to publish graduation rates for Pell grant recipients in 2008, and in doing so, revealed a gap in graduation rates among Pell grant recipients as compared with non–Pell grant recipients.

When SCHEV began reporting these data many state policy makers were not interested, because they had little interest in collecting or studying data on federal program recipients that the federal government demonstrated no interest in collecting. However, over time SCHEV administrators were able to convince state policy makers that the graduation gap between Pell grant recipients and nonrecipients represented more than a performance issue for federal program recipients. Rather, because Pell grant recipients are ostensibly equal to nonrecipients in every other way, the gap represents an issue of access to credentialing within state institutions. Therefore, graduation rates of Pell grant recipients as well as other performance measures such as time and credits to completion, have become measures of access and affordability, as well as performance metrics.

## Advocating for Student Veteran Success: A Data Collection Strategy

In an ideal world, statewide longitudinal data collection would provide the information required to identify, promote, and support pathways for student veteran success. Identifying student veterans, tracking certain performance measures, and describing the amounts and types of financial need are essential to the discovery and evaluation process. The following section provides recommendations for a strategic, efficient approach to obtaining this information from institutional data systems for statelevel aggregation and reporting.

**Identifying Student Veterans.**    In Virginia, all current data collection on military students (active, reserve, and veterans) and their families is performed through the lens of specific types of financial aid distribution. However, the identification of all military personnel within institutional data systems would provide essential information about scale, establish the basic indicators necessary to track individual progress, and facilitate the detection of relationships between veteran status, student success, and covariables. The Common Education Data Standards (n.d.) treats active military, veteran, and military branch identifiers as basic demographic data. Additional information on combat experience and dates or length of service may allow for additional targeting of subcohorts and programming, as well as identification and targeting of potential risk factors.

**Describing Financial Need.**    Once a basic count and demographic description of student veterans is in place, a more robust description of their financial need is required. Federal need calculations are based on whether student veterans qualify for the G.I. Bill and are using those benefits; this aligns with the Common Education Data Standards (n.d.), which include indicators for veteran benefit status and type in the financial aid data-collection schema. However, additional information is required to understand if those benefits are meeting financial need. G.I. Bill benefits can be studied in relation to total cost of attendance. Documenting any supplementation with federal and/or private student loans would shed additional light and suggest a spectrum of implications related to student debt outcomes. Finally, the family status of the student veteran—and whether he or she (and his or her family) is living above or below the poverty line—has a known impact on student success. Understanding these nuances would help guide the creation of programming to address student veteran needs.

**Measuring Success and Identifying Sticking Points.**    Identifying and tracking performance outcomes is necessary to evaluate the impact of policies and programming. Common performance outcomes include retention, time and credits to completion, transfer and graduation rates, and award type. Timing and circumstances surrounding stop-outs (defined as noncontinuous patterns of enrollment within the same institution within the 10 years), dropouts (defined as a failure to return to an institution within a 10-year period), and other delays in completion could help institutions target barriers to institutional effectiveness and student success.

## Meaningful Analyses for Statewide Student Veteran Data

Once the appropriate data elements are present in institutional data systems, they can be aggregated at the institutional and state level to show trends in and across institutions (and, in some cases, sectors). Certain analytic and reporting structures are more effective for comparing outcomes, displaying student flow, and defining student needs.

**Head-Count Reporting.** Head-count reporting represents a simple counting process meant to convey tangible outcomes. This approach allows for basic comparisons over time and across institutions in terms of student veteran demographics, enrollment, and straightforward performance measures (e.g., retention and graduation rates). The presence of demographic data allows for more precision in monitoring trends in student veteran data.

**Cohort Life-Cycle Analysis.** Modeled after the Student Learning Progress Model (Rice, Coughlin, & Holmes, 2012), the SCHEV cohort life-cycle analysis tracks student progress term by term for 10 years, indicating every time the student initiates an enrollment in a new institution as an undergraduate. It captures demographics, prior experience, enrollment, subsequent transfer, transfer enrollment, stop-out rates, and dropout rates. These data facilitate demonstrations of patterns of student behavior broken down into general cohort classifications (such as full-time and part-time, first-time enrolled and new transfer students). However, it also allows for the display of behavior across demographic and subcohort groups. Previously studied subcohorts include financial aid recipients, those with families with financial need, standardized test scores, or intensity of course load at the time of entry.

**Credential Production Reporting.** As part of a more detailed examination of performance outcomes, the raw numbers of student veterans receiving awards can be divided into degrees, credit-based certificates, and non-credit workforce credentials. Demonstrating the relationship between the awarded credentials and military occupational specialties would speak to alignment between military training and higher education pathways. Finally, metrics that provide information about the efficiency of the process, including time to completion, credits to completions, and college credit received for previous military experience would provide clues to sticking points in the process between enrollment and graduation.

**Outcomes Beyond Credentials Analysis.** SLDS allow for an expansion of thinking on performance outcomes beyond the credential. Partnerships between postsecondary and workforce sector agencies allow for tracking of employment, wage outcomes, the accessing of unemployment benefits, and other workforce-related outcomes.

## Conclusion

Statewide longitudinal data systems should do more than quantify and provide evidence of accountability with state and federal programming. The decision to identify and track any student group—including student veterans—carries with it the implicit willingness to acknowledge and attempt to address student needs and any gaps in access or performance that become apparent. Advocacy for student veterans requires more than counting students, although this is an essential first step in the process. Financial need, beyond Post-9/11 G.I. benefits, must be understood. Basic performance measures, such as time and credits to completion; retention, transfer, and graduation rates; and program and degree type can be used to indicate gaps or sticking points for student veterans within the educational pipeline. SLDS provide opportunities to expand the study of student veteran outcomes beyond graduation to wages and employment.

So much of what can be achieved in terms of data collection comes down to the purpose and content of state policy and the motivations and perceptions of state policymakers. Despite the robust nature of its postsecondary LDS and VLDS, the State Council of the Higher Education for Virginia cannot identify or count student veterans within its colleges and universities, let alone comment on basic performance measures. Short of a full match of data between SCHEV and the U.S. Department of Veterans Affairs, much of the decision to move toward identification of student veterans will have to take place at the institutional level. Once student veterans are being identified by the institutions, SCHEV will be able to make connections between affordability, access, and student veteran performance much in the same way it did for Pell grant recipients in 2008.

## References

Cate, C. A. (2014). *Million Records Project: Research from Student Veterans of America*. Retrieved from https://studentveterans.org/images/Reingold_Materials/mrp/download-materials/mrp_Full_report.pdf

Common Education Data Standards. (n.d.). *Domain entity schema*. Retrieved from https://ceds.ed.gov/domainEntitySchema.aspx

Commonwealth of Virginia. (2016). *Virginia code*. Retrieved from http://law.lis.virginia.gov/vacode

Education Commission of the States. (2016). *50 state comparison: State longitudinal data systems*. Retrieved from http://www.ecs.org/state-longitudinal-data-systems/

Ewell, P. (1995). Working over time: The evolution of longitudinal student tracking data bases. *New Directions for Institutional Research, 87*(3), 7–19.

McBain, L., Kim, Y., Cook, B., & Snead, K. (2012). From soldier to student II: Assessing campus programs for veterans and service members. Retrieved from http://www.

acenet.edu/news-room/Documents/From-Soldier-to-Student-II-Assessing-Campus-Programs.pdf

Office of Federal Student Aid. (n.d.). *Federal Pell grants.* Retrieved from https://studentaid.ed.gov/sa/types/grants-scholarships/pell

O'Herrin, E. (2011). Enhancing veteran success in higher education. *Peer Review, 13*(1). Retrieved from https://www.aacu.org/publications-research/periodicals/enhancing-veteran-success-higher-education

Student Veterans of America. (2014). *Annual report.* Retrieved from http://studentveterans.org/images/SVA-AnnualReport2014.pdf

Radford, A. (2009). *Military service members and veterans in higher education: What the new GI Bill may mean for postsecondary institutions.* Washington, DC: American Council on Education.

Rice, G., Coughlin, M. A., & Holmes, E. (2012). *Student learning progress model: Beta test summary report.* Retrieved from https://www.airweb.org/AboutUs/History/Documents/Rice-Student%20Learning%20Progress%20Model.pdf

U.S. Department of Education. (2009). *State longitudinal data system.* Retrieved from http://www2.ed.gov/programs/slds/factsheet.html

U.S. Department of Education. (2015). *State longitudinal data systems, glossary.* Retrieved from https://slds.grads360.org/#communities/pdc/documents/8541

VLDS. (n.d.). *Insights.* Retrieved from http://vlds.virginia.gov/insights

*Tod Massa is a United States Army veteran and current director of policy research and data warehousing for the State Council of Higher Education for Virginia.*

*Laura Gogia is the business intelligence liaison for the Virginia Statewide Longitudinal Data System for the State Council of Higher Education for Virginia.*

7

*The final chapter in this issue provides a summary of the key ideas presented throughout the issue and offers recommendations for future research and practice as related to studying and serving veterans in higher education.*

# Conclusion and Final Thoughts

*Kevin Eagan, Lesley McBain, Kevin C. Jones*

This chapter illustrates how institutional research (IR) professionals can be involved in the creation and/or modification of high-quality programs for student veterans, with particular attention paid to the importance of accurate data regarding this growing population of nontraditional students. Suggestions from authors within this issue are summarized and recommendations for future research and institutional research practice are made.

The breadth of topics addressed in the preceding chapters provide a sense of the many significant issues facing institutional researchers and other higher education stakeholders interested in improving data collection on the military-affiliated student population. As Chapter 1 noted, the history of veterans and other military-affiliated students in postsecondary education dates back decades; however, such students remain a historically understudied population in higher education research, with a lack of theoretical models designed specifically for them in mind. What, then, can be done going forward to address these gaps in data and methodology in order to study this population more effectively?

To begin, Chapter 2 discussed how existing student development models do or do not fit this population, leading to the necessity of making assessment and student service choices for military-affiliated students based on researching and assessing their lived experiences rather than solely relying on theories previously developed to address the maturation and individuation processes of a traditional (in both age and experience) civilian student population. Whether this leads to taking lessons from the for-profit sector and its focus on adult students, or to modifying assessment practices and research models, or to both, are areas for future research.

We recommend that a common taxonomy for military-affiliated students should be adapted. As discussed in Chapters 3 and 4, the subpopulations contained in the term "military-affiliated student population" are *not* identical. Education researchers and practitioners attempting to design effective programs and services for the benefit of these students need both better conceptual models (as Chapter 2 discussed) and more accurate data. Chapter 6 examines state-level data system collection of student veteran data, focusing on Virginia as an example, and suggests ways in which such aggregated data can be analyzed at both the state and institutional level.

As Chapter 5 addressed, the majority of student veterans study in the private for-profit sector—one that is difficult to research because of its inherent contradiction of simultaneously existing as a collection of for-profit entities deriving considerable financial benefit from federal funds and as educational providers. As a result, the questions that have been raised over many years about educational quality and student services are more difficult to answer because data are not available. Historically, this sector has done more marketing and outreach to the military-affiliated population than either the private nonprofit or public sectors of higher education, and the possibility exists for researchers (both institutional and academic) and policymakers to learn from the for-profit sector's position at the forefront of military-affiliated student education.

The chapters as a whole offer multiple points to consider. One crucial to institutional researchers is simply getting the nuanced data elements *correct* for the multiple subpopulations that make up the military-affiliated student population. Active-duty service members attending part-time in their off hours are *not* the same as veterans attending either full- or part-time after having fulfilled their military commitment, and they should not be lumped into the same sample data as "student veterans." Nor are dependent students using their parents' transferred Post-9/11 G.I. Bill benefits—an entirely new subpopulation created by this iteration of the G.I. Bill—the same as either their veteran parents or their active-duty service member peer students. The fact that many students within the military-affiliated student subpopulation have attended multiple institutions and thus are left out of the traditional first-time, full-time degree-seeking student category is another challenge facing institutional researchers who seek to collect and analyze data on this population. Understanding these nuances and being able to find, label, and distill data that addresses them is key to accurate analysis leading to better programs and services.

Finally, the broad issue of bridging the civilian–military gap in American postsecondary education with better data and research ties these threads together. Civilian institutional researchers and other stakeholders (e.g., faculty, administrators, and policy makers) need to understand better the differences *and* similarities of military-affiliated students as they collect data that inform policy and practice related to these students. Although addressing ways to gain cultural competency when dealing with military-affiliated stakeholders is beyond the scope of this volume, institutional researchers can look to the cultural elements embodied in the chapters dealing with specific data elements to assist them.

NEW DIRECTIONS FOR INSTITUTIONAL RESEARCH • DOI: 10.1002/ir

In the end, military-affiliated students are not so much an emerging population as one emerging from the shadows of American postsecondary education with the advent of the Post-9/11 G.I. Bill. Collecting data on them with care, and with cultural sensitivity, is necessary to assist them in succeeding in colleges and universities across the nation.

KEVIN EAGAN is assistant professor in residence, Graduate School of Education and Information Studies; director, Cooperative Institutional Research Program (CIRP); and managing director, Higher Education Research Institute (HERI) at the University of California, Los Angeles.

LESLEY MCBAIN is an assistant director of research and policy analysis at the National Association of College and University Business Officers (NACUBO).

KEVIN C. JONES, a former Marine, is director of strategic planning and assessment, Office of Institutional Research, Effectiveness, and Planning, at Polk State College.

# INDEX

Abell, P., 68
Abes, E. S., 27
Abrams, R. M., 11, 12
Ackerman, R., 17, 23, 24, 25, 27, 35, 36, 37, 59
Adaptive Military Transition Theory (AMTT), 30–34; model phases, 31; transition variations, 32–34
Adelman, C., 54
Altschuler, G., 12
American Council on Education, 44
Analyses of variance (ANOVA), 62
Anderson, J. L., 25
Appenzeller, G. N., 18
Armed Forces Qualification Test, 15
Astin, A., 35

Bean, J., 23, 24, 34, 35, 37
Beginning Postsecondary Student (BPS), 7, 59
Bennett, D., 79, 80
Bennett, M. J., 12, 13, 16
Berger, J., 23, 29, 34, 37
Berger, J. B., 24
Bidwell, C., 37
Blair, J., 14
Blumin, S., 12
Bound, J., 12, 13
Braxton, J. M., 23, 24
Britt, T. W., 18
Brown, E., 17
Brown, P. A., 17
Burke, P. J., 26
Byman, D., 17

Cabrera, A., 23
Call, V. R. A., 14
Castañeda, M., 24
Castro, C. A., 18
Cate, C. A., 8, 87, 89
Cawthon, T., 24, 25, 36
Chandrasekaran, R., 76
Chartrand, J., 24
Chickering, A. W., 24, 25
Clark, D. A., 13

Cohen, A., 59
Cohen, J., 13, 14, 15
Cohort default rate (CDR), 78
Cole, J. S., 33
Coley, J., 13, 14, 15, 16, 17, 33
Coll, J. E., 51
Coll, L. C., 51
Combat Veteran Conceptual Identity Model (CVCIM), 26–29
Conant, J. B., 16
Cook, B., 33, 35, 36, 59, 87
Cook, B. J., 16
Cooperative Institutional Research Program's (CIRP), 8
Coughlin, M. A., 93
Cramer's V, 65, 66
Crose, J. M., 16

Daly, D. D., 43, 58
Deaux, K., 27
Deming, D., 80
Deming, D. J., 75
Diamond, A., 23, 41
Diamond, A. M., 30, 36, 38
DiRamio, D., 17, 23, 24, 25, 26, 27, 35, 36, 37, 59, 76
Doubler, M. D., 11, 12
Doyle, W. R., 23

Eagan, K., 9, 97, 99
Eighmey, J., 59
Erikson, E., 24
Ewell, P., 88

Farrell, E., 12
Fiedler, R., 80
Field, A., 62, 63
Field, K., 12
Fishback, S., 27
Fleming, D., 24, 25, 36
Fox Garrity, B., 54, 80
Fox Garrity, B. K., 43, 58, 75, 85
Fredericksen, N., 16
Freeland, R., 12
Fusch, D., 48